UN-WORRIED BRAIN

Achieve More, Stress Less
And Turn Worry into Action
with Practical Brain Science

THE UN-WORRIED BRAIN
Achieve More, Stress Less and Turn Worry Into Action with
Practical Brain Science

For more great content, please visit the website:
braincoachbrad.com

THE UN-WORRIED Brain: Achieve More, Stress Less and
Turn Worry Into Action with Practical Brain Science
978-0-9968551-0-5

B.C. Allen Publishing: Books That Change Lives
(October 2015)

Publisher President: B. C. Allen
Cover Design and Layout: Olivia Storm
Editorial Team Lead: B. C. Allen

To Norah, Jake, Caleb, Mom, and Dad: You are deeply embedded in my brain, but even more deeply in my heart.

TABLE OF CONTENTS

THE UN-WORRIED BRAIN

SECTION ONE

INTRODUCTION AND PRINCIPLES

CHAPTER ONE

A SHOE, YOUR BRAIN, AND THIS BOOK

As I write the words on this page, there is a shoe on my desk. It's helping my brain.

If you are committed to wiping out worry, stress, and anxiety in your life, take one of your shoes off right now and put it on your desk. If there is no desk in front of you, then put it on the nearest bookcase, or just hold it out in front of you with one hand as you hold this book with the other.

Does this sound ridiculous? It very well may be, but it works. Which matters more to you? Are you willing to let your pride get in the way of your happiness and achievement?

This book will help you discover practical and very playful strategies for changing your brain in order to wipe out worry, stress, and anxiety. In it you will learn what you need to know about your brain to make immediate changes that will bring you the stress-free achievement you want.

One of the first things you will learn is that your brain is constantly processing all the sensory information it receives in order to prioritize it. Why? It is identifying anything important enough for an immediate response, anything that will affect your survival. Most of that information never makes it to your conscious awareness, but it is getting processed nonetheless.

Have you put your shoe on your desk yet?

If you have, then your brain is processing that information differently than everything else, because it is an anomaly, an unusual occurrence, and your brain wants to know, "what does it mean?" and "what should I do about it?" In the next moments, as you read these words with that shoe in your visual field, your brain will be repeating that process over and over. "What's that shoe doing on my desk? Oh, yes, I put it there because Brain Coach Brad challenged me to demonstrate that I was committed to wiping out worry, stress, and anxiety in my life." As this happens, your brain is constructing a new neural network (more about that later) that connects the presence of that shoe with your commitment. In so doing, it allows you to access that commitment much more easily than ever before.

I know this is not the first book you've read in order to improve your life. If you are like most people, you read those other books but didn't follow through, didn't do all the exercises and didn't practice on your own. Those experiences have created patterns, wiring, in your brain. To be successful with this book, or any effort to reduce and even eliminate the unproductive worry, stress, and anxiety in your life, you have to change that wiring. Your shoe can help you do it.

Pick up your shoe in your hand. Feel the heft of it. Maybe notice the traces of dirt on the sole. See it as you never have before. This shoe can be the entry into a new world, a world in which you understand how your brain works, and use that understanding to wipe out old habits of worry, stress, and anxiety. Think just for a moment about what your life will be like when you can achieve, be productive and successful, while leaving behind unproductive and unhelpful worry, stress, and anxiety. The shoe becomes a symbol of your commitment to these outcomes. The shoe is your first strategy for becoming the high-achieving, worry-free you.

As long as you can see it, even out of the corner of your eye, it will be affecting your brain. If you stray for a moment from your focus on these words, or consider not going ahead with your full effort, you will find that you suddenly become aware of your shoe. With that awareness, you have a choice.

In that moment, your opportunity is clear to you. You've taken the first step toward the confident, successful, and happy life that you desire. Will you take the next? You then have the choice to return your focus to this book, follow the exercises, and begin to change your old unhelpful habits.

If your dreams are important to you, get your shoe on that desk! Or put it on your head for all I care! (Even though you can't see it, your brain can feel its weight and, you must admit, it's pretty unusual for you to have a shoe on your head.) Now join me on your new journey to be free of unhelpful and unproductive worry, stress, and anxiety. You, and your shoe, are on your way!

CHAPTER TWO

INTRODUCTION

Your first steps on this journey will be in the footsteps of a client of mine, Jessica, another stressed-out high achiever who learned the hard way that stress, worry, and anxiety are barriers, not benefits, on the path to truly fulfilled success.

Imagine this: you are a young, high achiever entering graduate school at a prestigious university in your chosen field. This is a high water mark in your already ascendant career arc. You have arrived at this moment through years of last-minute work and late hours, fueled and driven by deadlines, overwhelming stress, worry, and moments of outright anxiety. But you are here, at this peak of achievement! Given your patterns up to this point, you naturally have some worries about moving across the country and competing against other top students, but you use those feelings to drive you to prepare even more diligently. You remind yourself, too, that your very supportive boyfriend will be following you shortly, and together you will soar to new heights of success.

That sounds wonderful, doesn't it? Or can you already see the potential challenges? What will happen?

Fast forward six weeks. You are sobbing into your couch, covering your head with your pillow. You received a "B" on an important paper and, despite everyone's reassurances, you can't stop thinking that you are going to get kicked out of the program at any moment.

You're not sleeping. You spend 16 hours a day at your desk but your work is deteriorating. When you turned to your boyfriend for support, he told you he's not coming; he can't handle the stress of the relationship. Your mom wants you to get on medication. You're anxious all the time, and you think you were never truly successful. The floor has dropped out from underneath you, you're spiraling downward, and nothing—not even the ever-increasing hours at your desk—seems to slow your fall.

Jessica's Journey

What happened with Jessica? The truth is that her challenges started long before she got to graduate school. Her prior successes had been built upon an unstable foundation. In fact, her successes had made her more vulnerable—weaker, not stronger. Jessica, like many high achievers, had learned to use worry and stress to drive her. And as these bloomed into anxiety, she accepted all three as part of the cost of success.

She had turned the helpful aspects of stress and worry into the painful and destructive cycle of anxiety. In doing so, she had wired her brain to expect that with bigger dreams would come more worry, more stress, and more anxiety. She wouldn't feel like she was really trying if she wasn't anxiously worrying about every detail. Then, when the demands of her life increased, she couldn't handle the intensified feelings. The greater the stakes, the greater the worry.

Is this pattern familiar to you? Are you an achiever who has come to accept worry, stress, and anxiety as a cost of success? Have you ever wondered what it would be like if your achievements didn't have to come at the expense of your sense of sanity or your personal relationships? What if you felt more happy, joyful, and "in the moment" every day?

"Is that even possible?"

That was Jessica's first question to me, and my answer was immediate: "Yes, you can develop an unworried brain—a brain that effectively uses worry and stress for greater productivity while eliminating the anxiety that gets in the way of success."

I knew it was possible when I said this, because I had done it myself. I had been the stressed out, anxious achiever (under-achiever, really), and had come to the point where I, too, thought I would have to give up on my dreams.

Delivering Pizzas Rewires My Brain

On my 30th birthday, I stood in line at Domino's Pizza. I had two Masters degrees, with honors, and in the previous year I had left a good job as a therapist in order to pursue an entrepreneurial venture. Earlier in the year, I had walked across burning coals, demonstrating to myself that I could do things that felt impossible. Despite all that, I wasn't at Domino's to order a pizza. I was there to apply for a job as a delivery driver.

I had faced the fact that at 30 years old, with a wife and a four-year-old son at home, I was not succeeding at my business. I felt constant stress, and I became so anxious when I imagined going out and talking to potential customers that I was avoiding sales situations. I was in debt and getter deeper every day. I had a dream to impact the world and to help people be happier and more successful. That's why I had become a therapist, and it's also why, after becoming frustrated with the traditional mental health system, I had left my therapy job in the hopes of making enough money to help more people. But it wasn't working. I wasn't making money, and most days I felt like a failure.

But not on my birthday. Not in line at Domino's Pizza. You might think that deciding to deliver pizza could only be experienced as another failure, but that would be to underestimate the power of the brain. As I handed in my application, as I later accepted the red and blue shirt of a Domino's delivery driver, and as I headed out for my first delivery, I felt like I was finally turning a corner.

I was right. I had begun to change the habits that were holding me back, and that was the most important step I could have taken. I had picked this job for three reasons: I was qualified for it, having delivered pizzas when I was in college; I could start immediately and begin to bring in money to support my family; and the job would give me close to 30 hours a week in my car, during which I would be listening to self-development audio tapes while driving. This last fact was most important, because I was determined to use this time to rewire my brain.

Earlier in the year, I had gone to a seminar where I heard Tony Robbins speak and followed him across burning coals. This was before he had traveled the world and helped millions of people, but he was already teaching the basic tenets of what he called Neuro Associative Conditioning, which is a practice based on Neuro-Linguistic Programming, or "NLP." These approaches were based on the work of successful therapists and reflected the new (at the time) neuroscience discovery that it was possible to change the brain. In other words, he taught simple tools that helped change beliefs, attitudes, and habits of mind so one might achieve greater personal success. I had hoped to use these new learnings to be successful in my sales business, but I hadn't mastered them yet. I saw the pizza delivery job as a way to bring in much needed income while giving myself time to learn the new strategies.

For the next eight months, I delivered pizzas five to seven days a week. As I drove, I listened to recordings of Tony Robbins teaching brain-based strategies. I changed my beliefs about what was possible and I learned to take control of my emotional responses. Most importantly, I took my first steps on a 20-year journey of learning how to change habits that were deeply ingrained in my brain. Many of the strategies I developed at that time were the precursors to what I teach in this book.

After the eight months, I left Domino's Pizza and took a sales job. In the first month, I became the top sales producer in the company. I duplicated that result the second month. I had wiped out my anxious response to sales situations and felt confident and capable. More importantly, I had learned how to change my emotional habits regarding sales, and I had learned to take the necessary action in stressful situations to help me reach my goals. What I had learned about habit formation I could apply in any situation. I became determined to use it to return to my original goal of helping people break out of their emotional suffering.

Over the last twenty years, I have taken major steps toward my goal. I have helped co-found a national behavioral health company and have taught hundreds of counselors strategies to help people overcome crisis and emotional suffering. Last year, in 2014, that company responded to almost 500,000 callers in crisis. And I have personally worked with thousands of such clients myself. After 9/11, I was asked to go to New York to work with NYPD officers who were dealing with post-traumatic stress. I have run virtual programs like my "30 Days to Worry Free Achievement" program that had attendees from six countries across four continents.

Most importantly, I have learned to translate research on the mind and the brain into strategies that can be used to break habits of worry, stress, and anxiety and create new habits of confident, successful action. You can learn to use these strategies just as Jessica and so many of my clients have done.

Ah, yes, what about Jessica? You followed her in your imagination into her pain, sobbing on the couch, before she called me. You may be wondering, "what happened next?"

Jessica followed the steps you will learn in the rest of this book. She learned the FIRE! process that enabled her to break her habits of worry, stress, and anxiety and begin to lay down new, productive habits. She learned to access excitement instead of anxiety in challenging situations, and used that to fuel herself. She learned new ways to reduce the emotions that had threatened to overcome her, and new focus strategies that allowed her be more productive in eight hours a day than she ever had been in 14-16 hours at her desk. This allowed her to have time to sleep and break the cycles of exhaustion and emotional overwhelm. Not only did she succeed in her graduate work, but she began a stable and rewarding relationship. Finally, she shared her learnings with friends and colleagues and had the satisfaction of watching others benefit from her experience. Imagine all this growth happening rapidly from an enjoyable understanding and application of practical brain science. Are you ready now to truly excel? Then welcome to the world of *The Un-Worried Brain*.

Your Ideal Outcome

Now that you have read some of the amazing results that come from applying the tools and strategies in this book, take a moment and think about what you would like to accomplish.

Which of these would you most like to reduce? (Put a checkmark next to your answer.)

Anxiety _____   Stress _____Worry _____

Who are you focusing on as you read this book? (Put a checkmark next to your answer.)

Yourself _____   Others _____

Self then others _____   Others then self ____

What specific goals do you want to accomplish with the strategies you will learn in this book?

Fast forward to the day after you have achieved those goals. Suppose you had temporary amnesia on that day and didn't remember that you had reached your goals exactly the way you wanted. What would you first notice? What will your life be like then? What would be the first clues that you had reached your goals?

1.

2.

3.

If you would like to share your ideal outcome and three things you would notice when you reached your goals, please go to the companion website of www.unworriedbrain.com. I would love to read them. They may also inspire other readers.

CHAPTER THREE

WHY WORRY?

Bobby McFerrin had a generation singing "Don't worry, be happy!" Pharrell Williams inspired thousands of people around the globe to create videos showing themselves dancing to his song "Happy."

Yet millions more people worry and feel stressed and anxious every day. Did you ever wonder why? Why doesn't everyone realize the truth of McFerrin's catchy lyrics:

"In every life we have some trouble, but when you worry you make it double."

Think about a specific time when you worried and felt stress. Ponder on the question—why did you worry? Why did you feel the stress? There's an obvious type of answer to that question which would focus on elements of the situation, the circumstances. But there is a deeper level of response which focuses on you. After all, not everyone in similar circumstances would have worried or felt stressed. Why did you?

Many of my clients have found the answers to this question to be very revealing. They realized that the worry and stress were fulfilling a need for them. If this is true for you then you will need to find other ways to meet this same need before you can sustainably let go of the present habits of emotion.

The answers my clients came up with will not surprise you. Virginia, age 44, realized that worrying about her adult children helped her feel closer to them. It also helped her feel like she was important at a time when she felt much less control and impact in their lives. She even realized that if she didn't worry about them then she felt like she was a bad parent who didn't care about her children.

John, age 28 and in a new sales position at work, acknowledged that feeling stressed and even anxious was a way to demonstrate hard work at his office. If he looked like he was calm and confident he was afraid people would think he wasn't working hard enough or was irresponsibly optimistic.

Nancy, age 60, could see that her anxiety made her feel dependent on her husband and this actually helped her feel more secure in the relationship. She didn't consciously believe that he would leave her if she was independent and confident, but she admitted that she had a sense of relief knowing that he, as a caring person, would always be there as long as she was obviously in so much need. These realizations helped her also acknowledge that her anxiety had become so much a part of her that she didn't know who she would be if she didn't constantly feel anxious. She didn't know what she and her husband would talk about it if they weren't constantly talking about her worries and fears. There was always something different to worry about, and she felt like they were in it together.

Think about the needs you may have met in the past through your worry, stress, or anxiety. Take on as a hypothesis that your brain wouldn't continue any habits that didn't meet important needs. Be thoughtful about the role these habits have been playing for you.

The next step for my clients was to identify new ways to meet the same needs. Their intention was to eliminate unhelpful and unproductive worry, stress, and anxiety in their lives. They knew that they would only stick with their new habits if they could still meet those needs. You too will need new and sustainable approaches to meet the needs currently met by your old habits.

Create a list of needs previously met in your life by worry, stress, and/or anxiety. Be as specific as possible.

For each identified need, generate at least three alternative ways you could meet it in a future without unhelpful worry, stress, and anxiety. Again, be specific, but also be creative. Challenge yourself to come up with very different ways to meet your needs.

Here is an example from my client, John, mentioned above. He identified actions he could take to meet the needs of significance and certainty that he had been addressing through his stress. He realized that he could meet the same needs in other ways.

Here's what he brought to the next session:

1. Take the time I've been using to complain about being stressed and use it to rest. That will give me more energy at other times. I can use that energy to improve my performance. I'll feel better about myself then.

2. I can adopt the belief that my optimism and creativity are my best chances for success. Any time I feel stress I can look for creative ways to reach my goals, coming up with ideas no one else will think of.

3. I can start a list of accomplishments and positive moments from my days. I can go over them each evening, looking forward to more the next day.

Can you see how each of those actions could help meet the needs he had been meeting through stress? Using these behaviors to help feel better about himself, more significant, and also more certain and secure in himself was a relief. That allowed him to use the FIRE! process to eliminate his unproductive worry and stress and keep it that way.

As you read on in the book, continue to ponder these questions. Come back and expand upon your answers. Make sure you have multiple ways to meet all of your needs. This will open you up for sustainable change as you move toward a future where you have replaced your old habits of negative emotions.

CHAPTER FOUR

WHAT'S ALL THE STRESS ABOUT STRESS?

The fact that you're reading this book in order to eliminate your old habits of worry, stress, and anxiety indicates that you realize that they are not helpful for you—that in the long run they are a bad thing. In this section, my goal is to help you realize that however bad you thought these habits were, they are actually a lot worse than that!

One of the amazing things about our current society is that people are constantly talking about the statistics on the impact of stress, and yet it is sometimes seen as a badge of honor. The mixed message seems to be this: "Don't be stressed. . . but anyone who isn't stressed isn't working hard enough and doesn't care." Tough crowd.

By choosing to read this book, you have made a commitment to real change. I hope you have demonstrated that by putting a shoe on your desk.

Use that symbol as a motivation to look straight on at the hard truth about stress. This will keep you motivated as you are finally taking effective action to address it.

In a 2012 Yale University study[1], researchers demonstrated that traumatic or highly stressful events, such as the death of a loved one or the ending of a relationship or job, are correlated with an actual shrinking of the brain. That's right, events that cause enough stress actually result in white matter loss in certain regions of the brain. The areas most affected by this shrinking are the prefrontal cortex and other regions responsible for regulating both physical and emotional processes. The loss of brain capacity here has a significant long-term impact on the ability to manage ordinary life circumstances. This in turn can cause ever-worsening stress. . . Scary, right?

This study was particularly important, because not only did it give us this bad news in a really dramatic fashion, but it also offered a solution: an understanding of how stress is intended to work in the body. Although all of the participants in this study had showed brain shrinkage resulting from these major traumatic events, the shrinkage was not consistent across all participants. One key factor predicted the amount of brain shrinkage—self-report of daily stress. The greatest impact was found in those who reported that, in addition to these particular stressful traumatic events, they also experienced life on a daily basis as stressful. This group reported that they "always felt stressed."

The study revealed that the brains of this group shrunk on average twice as much as those who reported the same major stressful events but did not experience daily life as stressful. Even more importantly, the second group not only experienced less than half of the brain shrinkage, but also experienced growth in other areas of their brain. This growth appeared to be a response to the traumatic events. This is consistent with other results in a field of study now known as "Posttraumatic Growth."

This probably fits with your experience, with your life, or with people you know. Some people experience major stressful events and then continue to show the impact of them over time, while others are impacted by those events in the short-term, but actually report that they have "grown as a person" afterwards. They say that their lives are happier and that they feel stronger. This book will help you to become one of those people.

That's the Brain – What about the Body?

While the shrinking brain is quite startling and may catch your attention for a moment, it's not something that shows up in daily life. Stress' general impact, however, is much more evident. It is estimated that more than 235 million people in America alone experience extreme stress every day. Studies have shown that long term, continuous activation of the stress-response system can disrupt major body systems, including the digestive, immune, nervous, and cardiovascular systems.[2]

Stress also causes relationships to fracture. More than half of those who report extreme stress also state that stress causes them to withdraw. The resulting isolation leads to a vicious cycle because of isolation's negative effects; a 2010 Brigham Young University meta-analysis of data from 148 studies concluded that a lack of relationships and social contact increased mortality by more than 50%, the equivalent of 15 cigarettes and six shots of vodka per day.[3]

The negative impacts are even more extreme for those whose worry and stress progress to full-blown anxiety. 83% of those with anxiety report that it negatively affects their work, a fact which is corroborated by multiple studies proving that anxiety interferes with cognitive functioning. Middle-aged men with anxiety are three times more likely to have a fatal stroke than those without anxiety. Anxiety also interferes with relationships, furthering the concerns about isolation I just mentioned.[4]

Are you paying attention yet? Probably nothing in the previous two paragraphs was new for you. However, if you are like most people who have had habits of worry, stress, and anxiety, you have learned to filter out and ignore these risks. If you don't know how to change the habits, then focusing on their likely negative impact just feeds the cycle.

So let's get right down to the solution: you can't become less stressed if you don't know what to do about it. That is the purpose of this book. By following the strategies in the chapters on the FIRE! process, you will be able to turn everything around. You will dramatically reduce your vulnerability to the risk of stress-related consequences. You'll again experience the joy of stress-free living. Your motivation will turn into action, and you'll become more productive than you have ever been before. All it takes is a little knowledge of neuroscience and some incredibly effective tools. So take that shoe off and prepare for everything to change.

CHAPTER FIVE

WHAT DO YOU NEED TO KNOW ABOUT YOUR BRAIN?

One of my all-time favorite compliments was when I was once told that I was "like Bill Nye the Science Guy, but for the brain!" I have always admired Bill Nye because of the way he has made science accessible and interesting to anyone. We are not exactly the same—I admit to being even more outrageous and playful than he is; I do carry a plastic brain around in my glove box and sometimes in my pocket—but I relate to the way he humanizes the sciences. That is similar to my own goal: to translate neuroscience and psychology research into strategies that make sense, strategies that you can use immediately to improve your life.

Focusing on that goal in this book, I have restrained my enthusiasm about the details of neuroscience and limited this section to what you need to know to make a difference for you personally. To learn more about practical neuroscience and stay up on my most impactful brain strategies, check out my website[5] and blog. Throughout this book, you will learn just enough about the amazing discoveries of neuroscience to be able to use the strategies of this book in a way that works with your brain instead of against it.[6]

How much do you need to know about your brain, neuroscience, and research to help you wipe out unproductive worry, stress, and anxiety? I believe you probably need to know more than you do right now. It seems that most people know more about almost every other part of their body than they do about their brain! Even more importantly, most people don't know how to use their knowledge, limited or not, to change the habits that are holding them back. Let's change that together right now.

Principle #1 - Neuroplasticity Sets the Stage

To do that, I believe you need to know certain very basic principles drawn from neuroscience. I have used these principles as the foundation for my work as a therapist and a "brain coach." I am constantly amazed as my clients apply these strategies and turn these principles into action in their lives. Many of my clients have even modified the strategies to better fit their own circumstances and personality. It is both humbling and inspiring. What a gift to help others find methods that really work!

To set you on your way, I will introduce three basic principles or concepts regarding the brain:

neuroplasticity, habit formation, and the role played in optimal brain function by certain emotions. My work as a therapist, life coach, and brain coach has been a 25-year history of applying these principles with clients. I have used their feedback and results to create ever more effective strategies for personal growth and development. I have a passion for reading neuroscience and psychology research with one constant question in mind: how could this material translate into a practical strategy for me or for a client?

No matter your background, your application of practical brain science should always begin with the concept of neuroplasticity. You may already be familiar with the notion. I consider it to be the most important principle of modern neuroscience. It is the assertion that our brains are capable of change and are in fact constantly changing. This concept has begun to sweep through the popular consciousness to such an extent that many people do not realize how revolutionary it is; this understanding stands in complete opposition to the view of the brain that has dominated Western science for the last 400 years.

Neuroplasticity, the brain's ability to change, is the explanation for some astonishing results: stroke victims with irreparable brain damage have regained lost functions because other areas of the brain have taken on otherwise lost functions; learning to play the piano changes the amount of cortical map[7] dedicated to your hands; if you are completely deprived of light for between three to five days, your visual cortex (the area of your brain responsible for processing visual stimuli) will be begin to process auditory and tactical sensory information; chronic pain sufferers have been able to reduce their pain through visualizations, and more.[8]

The optimistic message of this book is due entirely to the discovery of neuroplasticity and its implications for each of us. Brains—your brain, my brain—can change, and that is a message of hope. Moreover, as neuroscience research provides increasing evidence of the nature and structure of that change, it also provides clues and guidelines for translating neuroplasticity into strategies for what really matters the most to us as human beings— sustainable, goal-directed personal change that improves our lives and well-being.

I promised at the beginning of this chapter that I would restrain my wild enthusiasm for the details of contemporary research, and I will. I will keep it practical. The playfully insulting but incredibly useful KISS! advice fits here: 'Keep It Simple, Stupid!'

In the writing of this book, I have constantly returned to, one might even say agonized over, the question of what it means to 'keep it simple' in this context. Fortunately, there are others like me trying to simplify complicated ideas for popular use. One popular phrase captures the next vital bit of knowledge you need to be on your way to a worry-free life. It is this: "Neurons that fire together, wire together." [9]

To 'unpack' this phrase here, I will simply say that in order to have any experience, including the experience you have right now as you read these words, your brain must activate and engage a particular sub-set of your neurons. Neurons convey electric impulses through the brain.[10] Neurons connect with other neurons, and when an electrical current is sent down a chain of neurons, the brain is thinking or responding or processing information. In short, neurons 'fire off' when they send these electric currents, and these currents make up our thoughts and actions, unconscious and conscious. As they 'fire,' they 'wire' together and will more easily 'fire' together in the future.

This is the purpose for the shoe on your desk. The neurons responding to the shoe are firing at the same time as those neurons that fire with your commitment to changing your patterns of worry, stress, and anxiety. They are wiring together. As you see your shoe in a future situation, or even think of it, you may now be reminded of this commitment. You may also smile at the absurdity of the shoe, further increasing the scope of the network of neurons. Each further association strengthens the wiring of your commitment.

How do you get the wiring that you want, that takes you where you want to go, instead of the wiring you don't want? There are two factors that result in increased wiring—repetition and intensity. Repetition is obvious. Since neurons that fire together wire together, the simplest path to wiring is lots and lots of firing. And more firing. And so on.

If you had unlimited time and energy, you could change any behavior or habit by simply repeating the new behavior enough times. In the absence of unlimited time and energy for repetition, the second factor looms in importance. Emotionally intense experiences wire neurons together more than less emotional experiences. This makes intuitive sense. A traumatic experience wires neurons together more than a routine moment in a grocery store, for example. Likewise an extremely happy event. We tend to remember these emotionally charged events more than most, right? Now you have a basic understanding of why. The brain's firing of the way a crowd looked on your graduation day stands out because there was a lot of emotion in that event, which means more firing and thus more wiring.

This is important as you think about worry, stress, and anxiety. All three can be emotionally intense experiences, resulting in increased wiring. How do you decrease this wiring? By applying the corollary to 'neurons that fire together wire together,' which is 'neurons that fire apart wire apart.' Neuron connectivity is constantly either increasing or decreasing based on firing patterns. If you wish to change the wiring patterns, you must change the firing patterns and redistribute emotional intensity. In this book, I will regularly offer strategies of playfulness and celebration as alternative emotionally intense experiences to change your wiring. (And that is why I carry a plastic brain in my glove box or pocket—as a playful reminder of my neuroplastic brain.)

Principle #2 – The Importance of Habits

Habits are so important in brain functioning that even brain-damaged individuals who cannot form new memories can still build new habits.[11] Anything the brain can turn into a habit will be turned into a habit, thereby preserving brain resources for other activities that benefit from conscious awareness. As a behavior becomes a habit, there is a change in the brain circuits governing the behavior, and there is decreased activation in the prefrontal cortex, the primary area responsible for conscious deliberation. This brain reality shows up in the shouts of countless sports coaches who urge their athletes to trust their habits and to 'stop thinking out there!'

The ubiquity of habits seems to prevent us from recognizing that some behaviors are in fact habits rather than elements of our personality. In particular, the success of the strategies in this book is a result of the recognition that your particular personal responses of worry, stress, and anxiety are best thought of as habits. And, as habits, they may be stubborn, but are still changeable.

Ann Graybiel and her MIT research team have studied habit formation in the brains of rats, revealing patterns that explain our own habitual behavior.[12] Graybiel has discovered an area of the brain that changes as habits are created, and it seems to encode the entire behavior as a single 'chunk' instead of a series of actions. Think about the first time you drove a car—you felt like you were doing lots of different things, and you were. Now you probably think of it as one thing—driving the car—and this is a reflection of how it is processed in your brain. Graybiel and her team have also discovered that as one habit is replaced by another, the first habit's brain pattern is not erased; it is only inhibited from firing. If the second habit is prevented from activating (as Graybiel can do in the rat's brains), then the first habit will reactivate. Again, this fits with our experience.

The most important thing to know about habits for the purpose of this book is that they follow the principle of 'neurons that wire together fire together.' Repetition and emotional intensity aid in this wiring process. Habits are stubborn and will not respond to half-hearted attempts at change. Summoning up extreme playfulness is the best way I have discovered to catch your brain's attention strongly enough to open up the possibility for new habit formation. You will see that theme repeated throughout the strategies in this book.

Principle # 3 - The Role of Worry, Stress, and Anxiety

This title of this book is intentionally misleading. It is what my mentor Steve Linder calls a 'bait and. . . add.' It baits you in with the promise of an 'unworried brain,' but it actually offers even a better alternative—a brain that uses worry and stress to its advantage.

A key step in wiping out unproductive and unhelpful worry, stress, and anxiety is to realize that the words "unproductive" and "unhelpful" are incredibly important in this sentence. There are different kinds of worry and stress. Whereas anxiety[13] is always to be avoided, worry and stress actually have a positive role to play in the brain. Unfortunately, most people have developed habits of worry and stress that go far beyond their beneficial use. Not understanding the optimal functioning of the brain, they have unintentionally created brain patterns of uncontrolled, unhelpful, and unproductive worry and stress. Frustrated and unhappy, they are urged, "Don't worry, be happy," by well intentioned others, but they feel unable to comply.

As you think about worry and stress as brain and body processes that can be either helpful or unhelpful, you might benefit from a parallel. There is a very natural one: pain. People with chronic pain experience pain that has become out of control. It is no longer playing its proper function. They may reach the point where they wish they had no pain at all. Unfortunately that would be no better. Many people with chronic pain might think that they want to wipe out all pain in their lives, but a life without pain is actually not at all a safe life. Pain plays an important role as a warning signal to let us know when our body is threatened.

Similarly, worry is a part of our response to potential gain or loss, and it plays an important role by activating attention and action. Worry gets 'turned on' when there is an imminent potential loss or gain. In other words, worry tells you when it is important for you to take action in order to either make your life better, or keep it from getting worse.

Simply phrased, the role of worry is to lead you to action. Worry without action is very much like leaving your hand on a hot stove after it's burning. It continues to sizzle, but it doesn't do you any good. Productive worry is deliberation leading to effective action. In later chapters, you will learn how to optimize your effective action and how to turn off worry when it is no longer needed. You have already begun to determine how your habit of worry has helped you meet certain human needs. By addressing those needs, you lay the framework for new habits of only productive and helpful worry.

Our internal reaction to stress also plays a role in action. I distinguish here between outside stresses and our internal stress response. The stress response is a physiological response in which the body emphasizes certain functions and de-emphasizes others to best prepare for immediate action. This is why this response is often called the fight or flight response. The body prioritizes physiological functions to prepare you to either fight in a situation or to flee the situation.

In the stress response, your breathing gets faster and your pulse speeds up. Your eyes dilate, and your blood flow is pulled from the extremities and moved to the brain and other essential organs. The immune system and reproductive systems are de-prioritized, too. You may immediately see why it's so important to counteract long-term and chronic stress; the stress response is designed to be implemented only temporarily in order to best prepare you for action. Then your system is designed to return to a rest state, which allows for all systems to return to high priority. In the long term, constant stress has significant negative effects in your digestive, reproductive and immune systems.

Take a moment to assess your own use of worry and stress. Are you able to use worry to lead you to action that is followed by a relaxed state? Is your stress response always short-term and followed by calm recuperation? If not, you need to learn how to fire off new neurons, wire together new neurons, and build new habits. You need to master the FIRE!

process and harness the amazing power of your neuroplastic brain.

CHAPTER SIX

CREATE NEW HABITS WITH THE POWER OF FIRE!

The FIRE! process is named after the crucial generalization of neuroscience that you have already learned: "neurons that fire together wire together." We can take the word "FIRE" and use it as a way to remember the key steps to break the old habits of worry, stress, and anxiety and to build new habits in their place. There are four steps to the FIRE! process: FIND!, INTERRUPT!, REPLACE! and EXERCISE!

The first step is "F for FIND!" You can think of this also as the "Notice" stage or the "Become Aware" stage. This is the most important step; all of the subsequent steps depend on it. You have to begin by reversing the process of having "told your brain" to keep the process of worry, stress, and anxiety at an unconscious level. The entirety of the FIND! process is designed to give you a moment of conscious awareness, to pull the earliest possible moment of stress, worry, or anxiety into your consciousness so that you have a choice about how to handle it.

Once that happens, you are prepared for the next step: "I for INTERRUPT!" Just the noticing and becoming aware, in the FIND! step can be an incredibly powerful interruption process. In this book you will learn how to intensify the emotional power of FIND! by employing a conscious decision to INTERRUPT! the old process, which will allow you to break, and even shatter, the patterns you have developed. As you recall, it is the combination of repetition and emotional intensity that determines the extent of the wiring between neurons. The emotional intensity of the INTERRUPT! step allows you to rewire your brain more quickly.

The brain abhors a vacuum. Once you've interrupted old habits your brain is going to inevitably follow that interruption with something. The "R for REPLACE!" is the intentional process of determining the new thought, emotion, or behavior you are going to drop into the place of the old habits of worry, stress, and anxiety.

The fourth step is the one that makes this all sustainable. That is the step I call "E for EXERCISE!" This is the conditioning of the habit. It is the repeating of the first three steps with high emotional intensity until the feelings, thoughts, and behaviors that were initially a replacement are now their own habit.

The FIRE! process can easily be grasped through the story of a client, John, who had developed a habit of becoming stressed whenever he drove. His own characterization of the experience was that he was providing "justice" to "bad drivers." He would chase after drivers who had cut him off, or otherwise drove poorly, and yell at them. He had a Mercedes sports car that he had initially enjoyed but that had unfortunately now become associated with an extremely stressful experience.

John was reluctant to accept that his stress was a result of his habits, but became convinced when he acknowledged the level of anger he felt toward the other drivers. He had strong values of empathy and compassion and realized that those values were not reflected in his current driving habits. His actions of so-called "justice" betrayed his fundamental beliefs, so he took action using the FIRE! system.

He engaged the first step of the FIRE! process, FIND!, by training himself to celebrate whenever he noticed someone driving dangerously. He would then INTERRUPT! his old habits by pumping his fist in the air. The fist pump was a part of a Power Move (more about that later) that instantly helped him feel confident and determined. He could decide whether the other person was driving so dangerously that a 911 call needed to be made. If so, he would do it without feeling anger. If not, he would then REPLACE! his old habit through a visualization of a "lovelight," which was the visualization of a search light of love beaming from his heart toward the other driver. This was a much more accurate metaphorical representation of his values.

John focused on how much he hoped the other person would get home safely, without harming anyone, and he came up with a generous and compassionate explanation for why the person might be driving too fast. He followed through on the EXERCISE! step by practicing the first three steps whenever he was driving.

Very quickly he noticed that driving was fun for him again. He even noticed that he was "aiming his lovelight" at more drivers, even those driving safely, and he was looking at them with caring and compassion. He began to enjoy driving again, while noticing that he was generally driving more slowly and mindfully at all times. He noticed that he felt much less stress in other parts of his life, too, and realized that his driving habits had been stimulating a heightened sense of vigilance and stress throughout his day. After using the FIRE! process, he was happier and less stressed, allowing him to be more productive and effective. He had taken control of the wiring in his brain.

Now It's Your Turn

In each of the four major sections of this book, I will address one of the four steps of the FIRE! process. I will explain the purpose of the step and provide you with simple, but profoundly powerful, strategies to allow you to follow John's example. As you practice the strategies you will begin to eliminate the unhelpful and unproductive habits of worry, stress, and anxiety in your life. You will learn to use worry and stress appropriately, and find that you can take action and achieve success without anxiety. By the end of the book you, too, will have learned to rewire your brain.

SECTION TWO

FIND!

CHAPTER SEVEN

FIND!

It's already the zombie apocalypse, but nobody realizes it.

Sure, the common man-eating zombie abounds in television and movies. But there is a different kind of zombie that is even more prevalent—a zombie that eats more brains, infects more people, and terrorizes us in complete disguise. You, in fact, are one of these zombies: the unintentional "habit zombie." We all are. And that explains the necessity for the first step in the FIRE! process—FIND!

You now realize that stress, worry, and anxiety are habits. In other words, they are on autopilot, like the barely-conscious zombie wandering around with a single goal in mind—stagger after food. Like the zombie that lacks all self-awareness, it's almost as if you told your brain, "Don't bother me with conscious awareness. I already know what I'm going to do here." That makes it harder to catch yourself and change your behavior the moment the behavior starts. In short, that's what it is to have a habit. It's an unconscious operation. A zombie-like operation.

Therefore, the first step in building new habits is to create a conscious awareness of this behavior and the process that leads up to it. You do this by celebrating your awareness of the habit itself. In other words, temporarily create a conscious behavior of celebration every time you notice that you have started to feel worry, stress, or anxiety. Notice, celebrate! Repeat! Simple.

The Old Attempt to Change Habits – Beat Yourself Up

Using celebration in your efforts to notice and change old habits is effective, in part, because it replaces a much more common and less effective process of habit elimination: beating yourself up. In the past, you have probably attempted to change your habits. You may even have attempted to bring them to your conscious awareness in order to make the changes. Unfortunately, the most common way of attempting to change habits of worry, stress, or anxiety is through beating oneself up. Self-criticism, self blame, or anger are common responses when people notice that they are performing a behavior they told themselves to avoid.

There is a way in which this self-attack makes sense. It acknowledges the fact that people move away from, or attempt to avoid, pain. People don't like pain, and "beating oneself up" can be an attempt to use pain to change a behavior. Have you ever fallen into this trap?

It's natural, but there is a reason why it is ineffective. When you don't know how the brain works, then you give yourself pain in a way that actually makes the unwanted behavior worse. Think about the dilemma for a moment. You want to punish yourself for your mistake hoping you won't do it again. But you can only punish yourself when you are aware of it—not when you do it unconsciously. But it's a habit! That means it almost always happens unconsciously. The only time you are aware of it is after the fact. If you get mad at yourself, then you're not punishing the habit; you are effectively punishing the awareness.

If you do it this way, you are unintentionally teaching your brain to become unaware—to stay on autopilot—by punishing it whenever you become conscious of your unwanted habits. This is obviously counterproductive, and it results in even less conscious awareness of the unproductive habits.

A client once gave me a great metaphor for this. He said, "It's almost as if I had a dog who kept running away. Every time the dog came home, I would yell and scream at him, wanting to teach him not to run away. But my behavior was really teaching the dog not to come home!"

Similarly, you have been teaching your brain not to "tell you" (bring to conscious awareness that is), when you become aware of your bad habit. Your brain has learned that in these circumstances you are going to feel pain if you are conscious of your behavior, so it decides that it's best to keep the behavior at the unconscious level.

Your Brain Likes Rewards, So Reward It By Celebrating

The first step in a solution is to reverse the process—to practice celebrating every time you become aware of any signs that you are engaging in the habits of unproductive worry, stress, or anxiety. In so doing, you will reward your brain for bringing this process to consciousness. The brain responds even more powerfully to reward than it does to pain, and celebration is experienced as a powerful reward or reinforcement. It is an emotional intensity that you have associated with good feelings. Even if you don't yet feel like celebrating, the moment you engage in the act of celebrating it triggers off the neural network of celebration in your brain, and you will feel better.

This is an alternative to beating up on yourself. It teaches your brain to begin to look forward to the awareness of worry, stress, or anxiety by rewarding it with celebration. It creates a craving in your brain that will fuel the FIRE! process.

One important thing to keep in mind as you begin the FIND! process by celebrating awareness is that you may not immediately feel comfortable with the idea of celebrating in the middle of the moment of worry, stress, or anxiety. In fact, the natural interpretation might be that you are celebrating the fact of your worry, stress, or anxiety, or even worse, celebrating the fact of the situation or circumstance that you find yourself in. It's important to remind yourself in those moments that you are practicing something new with a very specific purpose. The purpose is to retrain your brain to break your old habits, and you are doing this by celebrating only one thing. You are celebrating the awareness—the moment that you realized you were getting worried, stressed, or anxious.

To take it to an even more playful level, you can even celebrate your awareness of any moment that you were about to beat up on yourself. Even if you catch yourself already in the act of self-criticism, you can change the pattern by celebrating the awareness of it, thus teaching your brain to let you know more quickly. Eventually, you will become aware of this even before you start the habit.

"How, Not Why?" – Mastering Your Internal Sensory Channels

The second step of the FIND! process is to bring to conscious awareness not just the fact of the habit of worry, stress, or anxiety, but the unconscious strategies that you have been using to create the emotions and the experience. There are three primary categories, or ways in which these experiences are created. I call these the "three sensory channels."

As you move through the FIND! process, you will be rewarding your brain for calling to your consciousness the awareness of the worry, stress, or anxiety, and also for shifting your focus to the method you have been using. To discover your personal method for creating worry, stress, and anxiety, you will be asking yourself, "How did I come to feel this way right now? What *internal strategies* did I use to create this experience?"

This approach stands in contrast to the much more common line of questioning used by so many people. They would be much more likely to ask themselves, "Why am I worried, stressed, or anxious?" The "how" question is much more useful and powerful than the "why" question. The "why" question only furthers the habit, because it directs the attention to the outside world or circumstances and away from the internal processes. The "how" question provides access to the internal strategy or process that creates the feeling or experience.

Paying Attention to What's Going On In Your Head

The three internal sensory channels used to create worry, stress, and anxiety are three of our five senses. We use a version of these senses internally. The first is your internal visual channel. You can think of this as your internal visual world: what you picture, imagine, visualize, or remember. Although these might differ slightly from one another, they are all elements of your internal visual channel.

Second, your internal auditory channel includes both what you say to yourself and your auditory memories. It includes what is often called "self talk" or your "inner voice." Along with their negative or critical self talk, many people also report that they hear a voice from the past, such as a parent or other authority figure. This voice can be just the tone they use to talk to themselves, or it can explicitly be the voice of someone else in their mind. I will refer to any of these occurrences as "your inner voice" whether or not it sounds like your own voice.

The final sensory channel is what we will call the "internal kinesthetic channel," and it includes the sensations or physical feelings that you have had during moments of worry, stress, or anxiety. The internal kinesthetic channel also includes the labels you have used to name or define these sensations. Although we can blur the boundary between the internal kinesthetic channel and internal auditory channel when observing the labels we use, it is important to focus on the difference between the sensations themselves and the labels we use to define these sensations. Labels could include "an anxious feeling," "feeling stressed out," "feeling overwhelmed," etc. Remember that the label is not the feeling; it is only your description of the feeling. How you name each feeling has a huge impact on how you experience it.

See, Hear, Feel

Asking specific questions will help you bring greater consciousness to the processes and strategies you use to create worry, stress, and anxiety. Once you first notice one of these feelings or the processes that lead to them, celebrate! Then deepen your understanding through questions. In other words, you will use the following questions to understand the strategies you have used "inside" in order to run the habits of worry, stress, or anxiety.

The first question will always be to draw attention to your internal visual channel, because this is a very common way to generate worry, stress, or anxiety. After you celebrate, you will ask yourself, "What did I just visualize, picture, imagine, or remember?" When you answer your question, be as specific as possible while also being patient and generous with yourself. You are only beginning this practice, so you may not immediately find it easy to notice and remember what was just in your mind. As you practice you will find that it becomes easier and more natural. Be sure to celebrate whatever you remember, celebrating that you were able to bring that to consciousness so that you can do something with it.

The second question is in the auditory channel. You'll ask yourself, "what did I just say to myself and how did I say it?" Make sure you include the second half of that question, and use it to bring to awareness the elements of your inner voice, specifically your critical inner voice. Internally, how you say something is equally important as what you say. It can have a huge impact on how you feel. Tone, after all, is just as significant as the content.

The third question is in the kinesthetic channel. You will ask yourself, "What sensations or physical feelings did I just have, and what did I label them?" Again, both halves of this question are important. Make sure that you are very specific and detailed in your description of the sensations and physical feelings. For example, "I have an anxious feeling in my stomach" is actually a label rather than a description of the sensations. The sensation might instead be described as "a fluttery feeling," or "tightness in the abdominal muscles."

Sometimes it is helpful to first label the sensations—"anxiety," for example—and then ask yourself, "What specific sensations in my body led me to think I am feeling anxious?" Some sensation-level descriptors have already been co-opted to serve as labels, carrying connotations beyond the sensations themselves. One example is "tense" or "tension." "I feel tense" is used to describe a feeling of stress rather than the tightness of the muscles themselves. In that case, that would be the label, and the description of the sensation might include "tight shoulder muscles, tight forehead muscles," etc.

Practicing the FIND! Questions

You can practice this right away. Go ahead and think of a moment recently when you were worried, stressed, or anxious. Although this will not be the most pleasant exercise when you begin, it is a necessary step in beginning to break the old unproductive and unhelpful habits.

Take a moment and remember that recent experience and even imagine floating out of your body now and floating down into that moment in your memory. Take yourself through each of the three questions below, remembering as much as you can about each of your three internal sensory channels.

What did I just visualize, picture, imagine, or remember?

What did I just say to myself and how did I say it?

What sensations or physical feelings did I just have, and what did I label them?

Write down your answers because you will be able to use them later in the book. When you finish, no matter how much or how little you were able to remember, celebrate that level of awareness. Take heart from your success. It will actually be much easier for you to use these questions when you are in the middle of the moment, having brought that moment to conscious awareness through the use of the Celebrate Awareness process. Remember, as you become aware of how you created an unhelpful emotion, you empower yourself to do it differently in the future. You take control of the direction of your habits.

After all, you're always going to be at least a part-time "habit zombie," acting automatically based on your habits. (You will learn more about the "part-time" nature of this in the chapter on mindfulness.) But every day you can do your part to stave off the zombie apocalypse by becoming a living, breathing contradiction – a self-aware zombie! You can choose your habits and only be on zombie-pilot with habits that you consciously desire.

Challenge

Ha! You thought this would be the next chapter, didn't you? But it is not. It is a moment of truth. I'm calling you out, my friends. Take a deep breath and be honest. Whether you need this challenge or not, either way you will win.

Did you do the exercise? Did you fully and thoughtfully engage in the exercise? If so, I commend you. Congratulate yourself and do a little touchdown dance. It takes true commitment and courage to step up and take action to change your life. If not, here is where you're being called out.

Chances are that this is not the first book that you have read to improve yourself in general or even to specifically break the habits of worry, stress, and anxiety. If you are like most people who read these books, then you've already developed bad habits. One of those habits might just be the habit of reading through a self-improvement book without doing the exercises. That is a self-sabotaging habit. It keeps you from your goals.

You already understand the FIRE! process, and you recognize that you can't continue your bad habits and still release worry, stress, and anxiety. You also know you have an opportunity to build new habits to lead you to success when reading a book like this.

You know exactly what I'm saying to you. Put down the book, go back, and do the exercise before you read the next section. I promise you I'll be waiting here for you, and so will your ideal future.

One of the benefits of doing this exercise is that you will experience the power of the FIRE! process. By fully engaging in the FIND! homework, you will not only bring the old habit to consciousness, you will also begin the next step, INTERRUPT! You will get a head start on wiping out the old habits of unproductive and unhelpful worry, stress, and anxiety.

If you skipped over the exercise initially and are now going back to it, then you can also get a little extra benefit out of this by realizing that I've helped you become conscious of another old bad habit. And you know what to do in the moment you realize that you are engaging in a bad habit, don't you? That's right: CELEBRATE!

So engage in an enthusiastic celebration. Go back and do the exercise. Then celebrate again! You are rewiring your brain, one step at a time. You might as well have fun doing it.

SECTION THREE

INTERRUPT!

CHAPTER EIGHT

INTRODUCTION TO THE INTERRUPT! STEP

Imagine that you are talking. You are saying something very important, and you hope a friend will listen attentively. You have been thinking about sharing this experience with your friend all day. It seems important, and you want the attention and engaging feedback your friend usually provides.

But what happens this time? You get interrupted mid-sentence, just as your story is reaching its peak. When you are trying to tell a story or process an event and you're interrupted, it's the worst, right? It totally throws you off course and derails your emotional energy. Nobody likes that.

Your habits don't like it either. When interrupted, your habits get discombobulated and aren't sure what they were doing. Your brain can't smoothly run the habit it was running, and it has to engage consciousness to figure out what to do next. This is exactly what you want when eliminating stress, worry, and anxiety. That is the purpose of the INTERRUPT! step—to throw a hitch into the smooth functioning of your brain's automatic non-conscious processing, right at the point where you were about to run a habit of worry, stress, or anxiety. In the INTERRUPT! step, you are pitting your brain against itself so it can better serve itself. Your brain has created a smooth operation of habits, using as little energy and consciousness as possible. This is great at maintaining the status quo, but it doesn't allow you to progress. To move forward, you must practice the role of the disrupter, agitator, radical—you must overthrow your old brain processes. This is the nature of progress; the old must be disrupted, and sometimes thrown out, in order for the new to be put in place.

A Few Hints

Why does the INTERRUPT! step come as the second step? Does the sequence really matter? Yes, indeed! By engaging in the FIRE! process's first step (FIND!), you've already begun to call your old habits up to consciousness. I emphasized how this was important because it gives you choices. But just being aware of that old process is not always enough to give you the power to fight against the momentum of the old habit. Some of these habits have been ingrained for years, so simply noticing them will not create enough force to overcome them. This is why INTERRUPT! is such a key step.

You can think of it this way – the INTERRUPT! step is like scratching a record or a Blu-Ray disc. Each time you interrupt a habit, you disrupt the recorded material. Like a nail through a record groove, interruption alters the established course of action. When you interrupt a habit, you alter the wiring, which makes it that much more difficult for you to act the same way again.

The timing of your interruptions is also important. If you recall the basic principles of the brain, in particular the concept that "neurons that fire together wire together," then you realize that any further repetition of an old habit reinforces the wiring of that habit, even if only a little.

This means that every repetition—every moment—counts! The faster you INTERRUPT!, and with the more emotional intensity, the better! At the same time, remember how important it is to celebrate whatever you are able to do. Therefore, remembering to INTERRUPT! at any time is better than not remembering. It's always worthy of celebration. So go ahead and INTERRUPT! any disempowering habit as soon as you realize that you have the opportunity. The celebration itself will add emotional intensity to your interruption process.

Lastly, as you think about interrupting old habits, you might be wondering what exactly you are interrupting. The main thing you are interrupting is your present experience, the experience that in the past would have inevitably lead to (or perpetuated) worry, stress, or anxiety. You are interrupting the process of thoughts, feelings, and behaviors that are part of the old habit. Eventually, the repetition of interrupting each moment of present experience will lead to an interruption of the old habit itself. By repetition, you will fuse in new wiring, new neuro-pathways, in replacement of the old ones.

Specifically, you are focused on interrupting your internal sensory channels. You are familiar with this from the FIND! process. You will have already noticed how the two steps of FIND! (celebrating awareness and asking yourself questions about your strategies of internal sensory channels) already provide a form of interruption. They do this because they change your focus from the outside environment and the potential causes of your sensations, and return your focus back instead to the strategies—the internal processes—that you used to create your experience.

Now, in the INTERRUPT! step, you will further the power of those initial FIND!-based interruptions. By engaging with each sensory channel, you will change the strategies themselves. Changed strategies equal changed emotions, and, eventually, changed habits. It is as if you are not only scratching the record and disrupting the old music, you are also simultaneously scratching in a new recording. In the next seven INTERRUPT! chapters, you will learn specific strategies that will guide you in your "scratching out" and "scratching in." Now is the time to start playing brand new music in your life!

CHAPTER NINE

SAVED BY THE CAVALRY!

Now that you understand the why, when, and what of the interruption process, you need to know how to interrupt appropriately and effectively. In the following chapters, you will learn a series of strategies to radically INTERRUPT! the two elements that lead to worry, stress, and anxiety. You will learn to INTERRUPT! your internal sensory channels as well as the habitual behaviors that you engage in. Once you work these strategies into your life, your old habits cannot continue to fire on auto-pilot. You will have more choice about how you want to feel in each given moment.

It can be helpful to have an example of how this step works. About 20 years ago, I went through a pretty tough time in my life. I was going through a divorce, and I was working in a mental health organization where I was continually helping people who were considering suicide. I loved serving these people and helping them make changes, but you can imagine the toll these daily conversations can have on a person. With these conversations filling my work hours and the difficulties at home filling my off hours, I was beginning to burn out.

I noticed during those months, especially while driving home from the office, that I was constantly stressed and worried. I would drift into worried thinking about my relationship, about my children, and also about the many things that were happening at work. Although I didn't know everything then that I know now about how the brain works, I knew enough to recognize that I needed to interrupt that process of worry—because it was only getting worse night after night.

It was then, while being on my own ragged edge, that I developed an INTERRUPT! solution that brought tremendous value to my life. I developed a strategy that I call the "Thought Cavalry." Part of the reason the Thought Cavalry is so effective is because it engages all three sensory channels simultaneously. You can think of it as flooding your brain with new visual, auditory, and kinesthetic signals that push out the old thought habits that were there before. Once you flood the brain with new stimuli, there is not enough room in your brain for the new, highly positive, emotionally intense information and the old information at the same time. Consequently, the old gets pushed out.

To do this, you will engage the visual, auditory, and kinesthetic channels simultaneously through activating neural networks that are already present in your brain—in particular around the metaphor of cavalry. This metaphor is particularly powerful for many Americans, and can be adjusted to increase its power for those less familiar with it.

The Thought Cavalry is a visualization, or in my turn of phrase, a "sensorization," because it involves all of your senses. It is a sensorization of your own positive thoughts coming to rescue you from the habits of worry, stress, and anxiety. Before you send in the mental troops, you must first engage the FIND! step. Let me explain by going back to my story.

As I was saying, I began to practice this step while I was driving in my car, worrying and fretting. I would first notice any moment when I began to worry about my children or my relationship, or when I began to feel stressed about work. I would then immediately celebrate that awareness in order to reward my brain for the awareness. Then, after feeling that positive charge of celebration, I would begin the sensorization by "calling" for the Thought Cavalry I would intentionally call up the memory of a bugle, the iconic sound that announced the charge of the cavalry. I would make the sound in my head as loudly as possible. You can imagine how that sounds. The "Doo-doo-doo, ta-doo, CHARGE!" You can hear that in your own head if you like: "Doo-doo-doo, ta-doo, Charge!"

Immediately following the bugle sound, I would visualize in my mind the cavalry coming up over the hill on their horses. I could picture the clothes they wore, the uniforms, the sounds of the hooves hitting the earth, and the look of intensity on their individual faces. These were my own positive thoughts, my own private cavalry, coming to my emotional rescue. The combination of the sound, which I would sometimes create out loud, and the visualization was very powerful. It easily interrupted two of my sensory channels with a flood of positivity replacing the negative thoughts.

The third step in this process was perhaps the most powerful, bringing in a strong sense of playfulness. Even as I was driving, I would imagine the feeling of being on one of those horses. I would hear in my head the "doo-doo-doo, ta-doo," and I would start to bounce up and down in my seat as if I were on horseback. I would imagine the cavalry swooping me away and providing me with my own horse to ride as we escaped the "enemy" of the unproductive worried and stressful thoughts.

Sometimes I would call a halt and counter-attack. We would swing back, and then we would charge down the unhelpful thoughts again. Immediately this would make me feel even more playful, relaxed, and confident. I would often find myself laughing at the power of my imagination, how intensive and vivid I could make the cavalry in my mind. The feeling of the horses going up and down and hearing that bugle left no room in my mind for the previous sensory channels that were creating the worry, stress, and anxiety. They were effectively interrupted and pushed out of my mind, their painful influence gone in the presence of my Thought Cavalry (To see me demonstrate the Thought Cavalry go to the book's companion website at www.unworriedbrain.com. I have a lot of fun with this exercise.)

As you can see, the core of the INTERRUPT! step is to engage sufficient emotional intensity to shatter the previous pattern and leave you with an opportunity for replacement. Naturally, that is the next step, REPLACE!, which we will talk about in later chapters. But first, in the chapters of INTERRUPT!, you will learn numerous strategies. Be sure to practice each of them and identify the ones that work best for you. In doing so, you'll maximize the strength of the full FIRE! process.

Bonus Points for Hilarious Images

I encourage my clients to think of their brain in playful ways. I often talk about my brain as a committee that is constantly chattering about me among themselves, doing their best to support me and to avoid annoying me. One of my clients seized on this idea and began to refer to his brain as a "committee of Oompa Loompas," from the old movie Willie Wonka and the Chocolate Factory. When he subsequently learned the Thought Cavalry strategy, he found himself immediately seeing his cavalry as a group of Oompa Loompas on ponies riding to his rescue. Although that may not seem like a fearsome force, it immediately brought about the desired effect. The hilarious image served to break through his negative thoughts instantly.

The moral of that story is clearly that we should never underestimate the power of a troop of Oompa Loompas! Also, be creative when you engage playfulness and it can serve as an instant release from worry, stress, and anxiety.

CHAPTER TEN

FADING AWAY CAN BE A GOOD THING

The Thought Cavalry is an effective strategy for simultaneously disrupting all three of your sensory channels. This is particularly important if you find that you commonly use all three channels to create your negative emotions. It is possible that as you go through the FIND! stage, you will discover that this is not the case for you; you may have a preference for one channel over the others. For example, you may be more likely to create a sense of anxiety by picturing something rather than by saying something to yourself. Or the opposite might be true.

In this chapter, you will learn how to target your strategies to particular sensory channels. You will learn three strategies; one strategy will address your internal visual channel, one strategy will address your internal auditory channel, and the third will address your internal kinesthetic channel.

Seeing the Past in a New Way – The "Visual Fade"

A few years ago I did something stupid. Well, maybe it was more recently than a few years ago, and I know there have been a lot more than one "something stupid." Face it, I have done lots of stupid things in my life. You, too, have probably done things you aren't proud of. That's a part of life.

I have had bad things happen to me. Lots of them. Again, you have too. Whenever possible, we want to learn from these things that we have done or had happen to us. At the least, we would like to let go of them and move on. Neither response is easy when any reminder of the memory brings negative emotions along with it. That is why this next strategy is so important. It helps us reduce the emotional baggage of past negative wiring.

This first strategy, which I call the "Visual Fade," is very helpful in correcting the worry, stress, and anxiety that comes from visually focusing on negative moments from your past. Though unintentional, visually recalling past experiences can drive intense feelings of stress and anxiety. The FIND! step will have helped you identify this pattern. This next INTERRUPT! strategy will help give you control over changing the pattern. Instead of feeling like you can't help but think about that moment in the past, and that you can't help but feel anxious in response, you will learn how to interrupt the cycle. You can even use it when you are focusing on imagined painful moments in your future. The Visual Fade process works with your imagination or memories and changes them to interrupt the process and diminish their emotional power. Follow the next exercise to train your brain to interrupt these internal pictures and feel confident and secure in any situation.

Get the Picture

First, call up a picture of the memory or a future event that you might respond to with anxiety. For your first practice session, you may want to start with something of only medium emotional intensity and then work your way up to the more anxiety-producing pictures.

Do you have a picture in mind? Good. Now, get specific about the details. Circle the word that best describes your experience of the picture. What does that picture look like right now?

Is it in black and white or color?
Is it dim or bright?
Is it fuzzy or clear?
Are the colors dull or vivid?

Trust your immediate instinct with these answers. You will get better with it as you practice. For now, go with your first responses.

Now Change the Picture

Imagine that you have a dial that controls these elements, then turn it up. For example, make the colors brighter. Pull the picture into greater focus. Pull the image closer toward you.

It is often the case that when you intensify everything in the picture, emotions or anxiety associated with the picture may also intensify. That is okay. Experience it for just a moment, and then let the picture or memory slide back to how it was before you intensified it.

Next, pull the image in for a second time. And again, let the image slide back.

The third and final time, as you pull the image in, imagine it bouncing off a force field that is protecting you. It just bounces off the force field and is pushed away! Make the old picture smaller and smaller as you increase the distance between you and the image. "Turn down" every element inside the image.

Notice the color, intensity, and brightness disappear as the image completely *fades away*. If the picture pops up brightly again, just repeat the process.

As a result of this, emotions originally associated with the picture most commonly reduce and sometimes completely disappear.

Fade Down and Go to Sleep

Five or six years ago, I was at multiple-day business conference led by Tony Robbins. The hours were long and participants were highly charged up at the end of the long day. This was exciting, but it brought with it potential challenges. Late one evening just before midnight, I was talking to another participant, Dave, who told me that he had years of anxiety related sleep problems that were even worse at the conference. "I don't think I've slept more than two hours a night this week," he said. "I was already struggling at home, where I was getting four or five hours, but this is ridiculous. I don't know how I can go on."

Dave told me that he was recently separated from his wife and he was also having trouble in his business. "I go to sleep OK, even with all the high energy here, but I wake up after only an hour or two. My mind is racing, and I can't seem to think about anything but my problems. The more I think about them, the more awake I get. Then I get upset and anxious that I won't be able to focus the next day if I don't sleep, which just seems to make it worse. I get more and more anxious. Even if I finally fall asleep, I am exhausted when I wake up."

Has this ever happened to you? When I worked as a therapist for police officers, I found that almost all of them struggled with this cycle of sleep and racing thoughts. They couldn't turn off their sense of vigilance and alertness, even when they slept. I noticed that my anxious clients had the same pattern, being unable to turn off their nighttime worry and anxiety. That is when I created what I call the "Auditory Fade" strategy, adapting it from the principles of NLP. It directly addresses the auditory channel. It is particularly helpful for cycles of sleeplessness and anxiety in the middle of the night, especially related to racing thoughts or a 'too awake' inner voice.

You can break this cycle by using the Auditory Fade to calm your inner voice and thereby reduce your brain's vigilance and alertness. This allows you to relax, thus creating a positive cycle instead. Follow the exercise below to become comfortable with this INTERRUPT! step. You can then use the strategy any time you experience racing thoughts and sleep disturbance.

Practice this now as you read, and then again at night. It is the same process at either time. First make sure you can hear yourself think. Listen to your inner voice. Whatever you are thinking, hear it as a clearly articulated monologue in your head.

Now, you are going to demonstrate that you have control over the inner voice. You probably have experience trying to stop the racing thoughts of your inner voice. In this process, you are going to first do the opposite. You are going to speed it up and make it louder.

You can understand this better with the metaphor of a stuck window. Instead of working against the resistance and trying to push the window down (or in this case trying to slow down your inner voice), you are going to lift the window open *first* (speed it up and make it louder). Only then will you shut the window (slow everything down).

You will do this twice. You will speed up the inner voice and make it louder. Then let it return to the initial speed and volume. Once more: speed it up and make it louder, then return to where you started. Go ahead and do that simple sequence now to practice controlling your inner voice. It doesn't matter what you are thinking about; this is just practice.

Good. Now you will do those two steps again, but add a third, slightly different, repetition. On the third time, you will again speed it up and make it louder. But then, rather than returning it to where it was, you will keep on slowing it... down... word... by... word. Let your inner voice get slower with every word you say.

Sometimes it is easier to slow the voice down if you add a visual element. For instance, you can see each word as if it is going across a screen very slowly. Allow each word to move across the screen before you allow yourself to say the next word in your mind. Some people find it helpful to imagine watching the words travel slowly down a spiral staircase. They picture the word moving step by step downward. What is most important in this process is that you speed it up first, then slow it all the way down. If the voice speeds up on its own, speed up with it—take it further than it wants to go, and then slow it back down, word... by... word. The key is to take control of your inner voice!

Practice it now.

"The Best Sleep of my Life"

I taught this strategy to Dave at the business conference. He was skeptical, because he was sure that his sleep and anxiety experiences were caused completely by his separation and business challenges and not by anything going on in his brain. I explained the principles and encouraged him to experiment with it. He agreed, saying that it would be helpful even if it only made things a little bit better.

When I saw him the next day he rushed over and hugged me. "You're not going to believe this," he began, and then caught himself and grinned. "Well, maybe you will believe it. It works! I couldn't get the hang of it immediately when I woke up last night, but I stayed with it, and after five or six repetitions I could feel my whole mind and body slowing down along with my inner voice. I woke up once more and was able to put myself right to sleep. It was the best sleep of my life!"

Dave learned the power of controlling the auditory channel. That was clearly the crucial internal sensory channel for him. Follow his example and practice until you can slow..... your..... voice.... down. You..... are...... getting.... sleepy. Hey, wake up and do the exercise!

The Kinesthetic Fade Process

The final Fade process is one of the most powerful strategies I have developed. It is especially useful if you have had anxiety with heightened physical arousal, such as a pounding heart or short shallow breath. Some people call these "panic attacks." This Fade strategy allows you to focus in on the sensations and teaches you to take control of them.

This is an internal process of clarifying and changing your feelings by engaging with the physical sensations themselves and with your metaphorical experience of them.

Suppose that you are having an experience that you describe as "feeling anxious" or "anxiety," and you want to change it. Follow the next six steps carefully and you can take control of the sensations. Then your entire experience of the emotional situation will change.

1. Start with your senses. What do you feel in your body that is registering as anxiety? Be very conscious of sensory input, labeling it at the most physical level possible. Ex: "There, that tension in my chest on the left side, and the fluttering in my center abdomen, and a pulsing sensation above my rib cage. . . those are all part of the sensory experience I am calling anxiety." Stay at the sensation level. This should be familiar to you from the FIND! step.

2. Move to what I call the "sensorization" level that is a visualization with all your senses) and ask yourself what the "anxiety" feels like at that level. This is still one level "down" from the "anxiety"

description level. You are describing the metaphor of the sensations. What does anxiety feel like, for you, right now? Butterflies in your stomach? Knots in your stomach? A sinking feeling in your gut? Electricity shooting through your body?

3. Take the most notable of the metaphors from step number two, the one that gets closest to the feeling, and embrace it. Imagine it happening inside you as vividly as you can, as if you were consciously engaged in the process. For example, feel the butterflies moving in your stomach. Imagine actual butterflies bouncing off the sides and getting more frantic, flittering from one side to the other. As you do, extend your awareness to your senses and imagine the "anxiety" sensation escalating with the frantic flight of each butterfly. Connect the sensorization and the senses. Feel more butterflies flittering, and intensify this sensation until you begin to feel more anxious.

4. When you can experience the feeling getting stronger/worse from step number three, pause for a moment and survey the combined senses and sensorization. Scale your emotions from one to ten. How intense is your present emotion?

5. After you get your rating, reverse the process in step number three. Slowly calm each butterfly, allowing them to rest on a beautiful flower. Then free them from your stomach, letting them calmly take flight. Notice any sense of reluctance or even a sense of joy? Which way is freedom from that old emotion? Let the butterflies fly peacefully away.

6. Extend the sensorization into the senses and let your body release the part of the "anxiety" that

isn't serving you, only keeping what you need. Let the rest fade away.

Apply this example to your own sensations. Be creative with the metaphor of the sensations and with your positive response. Call up all the resources you need. For example, in the previous metaphor of butterflies, you could access your positive characteristics metaphorically. You could call up the care and empathy you show to others and apply it to yourself in the form of a beautiful and nurturing parent butterfly who flies on a beam of love from your heart to your stomach and takes each frantic butterfly under her or his wing and calms it down. Or you could access your determination and perseverance to succeed in the form of a steady but gentle breeze that sweeps up the butterflies firmly and lands them safely on a perch. You are teaching your brain to lead the old programmed experiences of stress, worry, and anxiety into these new kinesthetic experiences. You are rewiring the feelings connected to these sensations! And (doing a little dance step and spin) you know what else you are doing? Being playful and having fun, of course!

You now have a specific strategy to INTERRUPT! each of the sensory channels. Use the information from the FIND! step to prioritize the strategies, starting with the one that will best address your old tendencies. Identify whether you were more likely to create your worry, stress, and anxiety through visual, auditory, or kinesthetic channels. Then begin to practice the appropriate Fade strategy. You will soon find that old "out of control" emotions now feel more in control.

CHAPTER ELEVEN

SCRAMBLES

What's even better than an effective strategy that can snap you out of your most painful critical moments? A strategy that does that while occasionally also sending you to the floor in a fit of uncontrollable laughter! If you have ever had a self-critical inner voice that you couldn't easily control, then you are going to love the Scrambles Strategy!

This is actually a series of related strategies. Scramble strategies provide a very powerful interruption with lots of emotional intensity. Scramble strategies are derived from Neuro-linguistic Programming, also called "NLP." The scramble process is critically important for negative or critical thoughts which can play an important role in the habits of worry, stress, or anxiety. If you have found that much of your stress or anxiety was driven by your auditory channel, then Scrambles will be very helpful. Scramble strategies are very playful and can create lots of emotional intensity, allowing you to change old habits very quickly.

The first step in the process is to identify the common phrases or "self-talk" that you have used to feel anxious. You may think of this as having a strong "critical voice." Common phrases might be:
"I am such an idiot!"
"Why do I always do that?"
"Why doesn't anything ever go right for me?"

Take a moment and return to your personal notes from the exercise at the end of the FIND! chapter. If you haven't yet answered the auditory channel questions, do it now. Identify at least five comments that you've said to yourself in times of worry, stress, or anxiety. If you are able to recall more than five, then focus on the five with the strongest emotional intensity. Make sure that you match the words with your most common usage. Notice whether you are likely, for example, to say "I am such an idiot," or "You are such an idiot." Capture your own inner voice precisely.

The next step in this INTERRUPT! strategy is also reminiscent of the FIND! step. You have identified the relevant words, and now you want to combine them with your habitual internal tone of voice. Say the phrases out loud as you have heard them in your head. Get as close as possible to the tone of voice used by your very own "critical inner voice."

Much of this process' power depends on the step above. Be sure that you have said every phrase in your typical tone of voice before you move on. You need the full experience of the power of the voice tone combined with the words.

Scratch the Record

The third step in the Scramble strategy is to repeat the negative phrases from above, but with a playful twist. Rather than saying them as you had heard them in your head, instead say them with the highest, squeakiest voice you can manage. Do your best to sound like a cartoon character. I often think of Mickey Mouse or Goofy. Make sure that the voice sounds as silly and playful as can be. You may notice that you automatically make strange faces in order to accomplish this voice. That's a good addition. Many of my clients report that the memory of my "bug-eyed" face from the scramble exercise helps them laugh whenever they practice. (To see me demonstrate a high-pitched voice Scramble strategy, complete with bug-eyed face, go to the book's companion website at www.unworriedbrain.com.)

The more outrageous tone of voice that you use, the more likely it is that you will activate a positive neural network. You are associating these formerly negative words with a very different set of neurons— the neurons activated by the playful voice. This robs the words of their previous negative intensity. You can even end up laughing instead.

There are several powerful variations of the Scramble strategy. Experiment with each to find the one that carries the most resonance or power for you.

Instead of using a high-pitched silly voice, experiment with saying the negative phrases with a sexy tone of voice. Use a seductive and "come hither" voice. Exaggerate it and have fun! Compare the effect of the high-pitched voice tone with that of the sexy voice tone. Use the one that best interrupts the negative emotions.

A third variation of the Scramble strategy is to sing the negative phrases. This can be powerful whether you are an experienced singer or are always off key. Either way, you will be changing the neural network associated with the phrases the very moment you put the words into song. Make sure that you practice this variation before you go on. (To see me demonstrate a singing Scramble strategy go to the companion website at www.unworriedbrain.com. You can even sing along!)

Engage in this strategy with high emotional intensity. Really "get into it!" The more intensity you use, the faster the brain will rewire your neural networks and make connections between the negative words and the new voice tones. The result will be remarkable. The next time that you automatically respond to a situation with your critical inner voice, you will be in for a surprise. You will find that you automatically hear an echo of the exercises you just did; your brain will repeat the phrase in its scrambled version and create a feeling of playfulness and fun. Enjoy it and celebrate it!

CHAPTER TWELVE

SKIP RIGHT PAST THE NEGATIVE EMOTIONS

When I was working as a counselor on a crisis hotline, I talked to people in really severe situations. Often people were crying when they called. They were so anxious and distressed that they were even thinking about taking their lives. It was difficult, as you can imagine, for them to be able to hear what I had to say. They couldn't focus on the words that could really help, the new strategies they could use to change their lives, when they were in the middle of that emotional state.

I spent a lot of time thinking about how to help them break out of their habits of worry, stress, and anxiety. Their emotions were so strong in the moment that everything else, even my voice, was blocked out. I realized then, even before I created the full FIRE! process, that I had to help my clients interrupt overwhelming states of crisis. Eventually, I learned to do that in a very playful and unusual way.

One day I was on the phone with a woman who was anxious, upset, and crying. Her tears muffled her voice, and there were long moments of silence between her responses. She didn't seem to connect with anything I said, and seemed ready to hang up still crying. Then I had a sudden realization of how to get through to her. I had been appealing to her emotions and to her rationality but there was a third path I had missed.

I suddenly said to her, "I'm going to ask you a surprising question. Are you standing up?" She was startled and through her tears she stammered out, "No, no, I'm not standing up." I said, "Would you do one thing? Would you stand up? I'll do it too. Let's just stand up." I could hear her sighs and her clothes rustling as she slowly stood up. Remarkably, her tears seemed to be cut in half almost immediately. She noticed it as well. Her voice sounded puzzled, as she just said, "Oh. Huh!"

As you are about to find out, your emotions are inevitably affected by your physical body and posture. If you were crying it would actually be quite difficult for you to continue to cry if you made a sudden change in your physiology and stood up straight. I used that insight to help that caller on the crisis hotline.

I said to her then, "Isn't that strange how that just happened? Even though nothing has changed yet in your situation, you were able to feel better just for a moment by standing up. Do you know how you would feel if you could take that standing up and move it further, if you could actually skip across the room right now? If you just skipped like a time when you were a kid and you felt so joyful and you skipped right now around the room, forward and then maybe backwards, and maybe with a couple of twirls? I know this isn't what you feel like doing right now and if you were able to do it anyway just once, you couldn't help but feel so much better, even before we start to change other things for you."

She immediately stopped crying, and began to engage with me. Just listening to me forced her brain to remember times when she was skipping and felt joyful, and that helped her feel better in the moment. She laughed, tentatively at first, and said, "I always liked to skip barefoot through mud puddles." She clearly had not remembered those moments for years. Over the next few minutes of our conversation she became much more aware of her resources and her options, and she came up with a solution to her crisis. She was grateful and hung up the phone with energy and enthusiasm.

I used the same strategies for years, with many distressed callers. To my knowledge, none of the callers actually skipped in that moment, but that didn't matter. I was still able to help them tap into the power of skipping, of using their bodies in a way that they had done only when they were children and felt joyful. Those childhood moments created neural networks that were so powerful that just vividly imagining skipping, as they listened to me describe it, changed their mood and their emotions. They felt better. In their improved mood, they were then able to move into learning the strategies that would help them overcome whatever crisis they faced.

I often remember those conversations. They taught me that such a simple technique can yield such powerful results, even in the most complicated and difficult situations. The power of this same technique has also been illustrated in my life. Some years after my time on the crisis hotline, I experienced some difficulties of my own. I went through a divorce and I was very anxious about my future and the future of my children. You may recall this from earlier in the book, because this is the same time that I developed the Thought Cavalry technique. I had learned to interrupt my worry, stress, and anxiety when I was in the car, but I needed to learn this at work.

During this time, I was working as a therapist and helping people again in very extreme situations. While I was working with my clients, I was able to stay focused on their needs, but the moment a session ended, my thoughts would sometimes drift to the difficulties I experienced in my personal life and I would begin to worry and feel stressed and even anxious.

One winter day I felt particularly distressed. As I was waiting for my next client, staring out the window at the gray sky, I suddenly remembered my time on the crisis hotline and the techniques that I taught the callers. If just thinking about skipping could impact someone so deeply, I wondered how powerful it would be to actually skip. I immediately put the idea into practice, and it changed my emotions dramatically.

I closed my door to my office, moved the soft brown chairs to one side, and I skipped around the room. I skipped around my desk. I skipped backwards. I even twirled. I used those 10 minutes in between sessions moving my body in a way I hadn't since I was a little kid, feeling the joy that I felt then when I had skipped. Afterwards, when I opened the door to my next client, I was in a completely different mood. All the worry I had about my personal life had temporarily vanished, and I was able to consistently bring my focus back to the client and to help him. He never knew that just moments before I looked like a little school child skipping around my desk.

This became a daily habit. On the more difficult days I would skip multiple times a day. Eventually it became so automatic that I would skip as I entered my office, and immediately feel free and joyful. The early morning skips set such a positive foundation for my mood that I needed less actual skipping during the day; I could just think about it and feel joyful and confident.

Several years later, as the Director for a national mental health care company, with many counselors working with me, I was known for taking the supervisor team for skips around the office. Skipping happened often enough, both with the team and on my own, that a particularly perceptive counselor came to me one day. She said, "Brad, I figured out what you're really doing with your skipping." I said, "What do you mean?" and she said, "I used to think that when I saw you skipping it was because you were having a particularly good day and that you were skipping because you were really happy that day. Then I realized that wasn't it at all! I realize now that on the days that you skip, you skip because you need the joy and the good feelings that you get from it. You are having what other people call a 'bad day,' and you immediately turn it into a good day by skipping." She was completely right. I had developed a habit of interrupting my habits of worry, stress, and anxiety through the skipping.

Don't Skip the Skipping Summary

You can easily apply this strategy, especially if you have noticed good feelings arising for you as you have read this section of the book. It is probably also true for you that the primary time when you have skipped in your life was when you were young. You didn't skip when you were sad or lonely, only when you were happy, and when you stopped skipping the brain kept that connection waiting there for you all these years later. That joy is just waiting for you to re-access it by skipping.

Skipping is a wonderful example, but it is only one of many playful strategies that uses the powerful connection between your body and emotions. In the following chapters we will further explore the amazing power of the physical body to interrupt habits of worry, stress, and anxiety.

CHAPTER THIRTEEN

THE POWER OF YOUR BODY

There's a very simple exercise that you can do to quickly demonstrate for yourself the power of the connection between your body and your emotions. Stand for a moment, read through the process, one paragraph at a time, and follow the steps.

First, stand up and hold out your hands, palms up in front of you at a comfortable height above your waist, shoulder width apart. You should hold your hands as if they were a balancing scale. Then begin to waver just slightly, lifting one hand and then the other, and also allow your body to sway just slightly from one foot to the other. Your hands and body should move only slightly, but perceptibly. While moving as described, read aloud the words in the next sentence and notice how it feels to do so.

"This is what I think."

Stop! If you have only been reading up to this point, and haven't yet physically done the exercise, then stop now and go back and do the first part. Remember your commitment to getting the most out of the exercises! Good. Now go back and do it.

Next, shake your hands and body out for a moment to prepare yourself for moving on in the exercise.

Still standing, place your feet a little wider than shoulder width apart and imagine that your feet are planted firmly into the ground. Lift your hands again, holding them this time as if preparing to do a Karate chop with each hand. Your hands should be straight and your fingers pressed tightly together. Your palms should be facing in towards each other at a slight angle, palms turned slightly down.

Lift both hands and chop down simultaneously. After you have done it once, return to the same position and do it once more, this time while again reading the words below, and noticing how you feel.

"This is what I think."

Did you notice any difference between your two instances of saying the words? Most people find that there is a substantial difference. Although no part of my instructions mentioned any change to your voice, you probably noticed a change in volume and pace. Most people find themselves saying the sentence more loudly and quickly, just because of the changes in their movements.

This happens automatically because of the neural network that is wired in your brain. The sharp and rapid movements of your body are connected to your voice tone and your volume unconsciously; when one part of that neural network fires and increases, everything increases.

You may also have experienced the second movement as a confident movement and the first as uncertain, or even wishy-washy. The physical movements of the first posture are a metaphorical extension of the sense of uncertainty. You were shifting from side to side. You were not stable or firm. This may remind you of times in your past. People who have habits of worry, stress, and anxiety feel a lack of confidence in many situations, and they don't realize that their physical body is reflecting that.

Power Poses

The physical body can do more than reflect your emotional states. It can actually direct them. When you take control of your body, which is often more accessible than your emotions, you are able to affect your emotions powerfully, quickly, and effectively. There has been increasing support for this in contemporary research. Amy Cuddy, a Harvard business professor, has led a series of studies into the relationship between the physical body and, in particular, physical posture, and emotions. Her studies are fascinating.

These studies were stimulated by Cuddy's experience in the classroom at Harvard. She noticed that female students received much lower grades in the classroom participation portion of the grade despite being equally qualified and prepared as their male colleagues. As she began to observe the students, she noticed that the male students sat quite differently than the female students. The male students tended to take up more space and sit with their arms and shoulders back and their legs spread. The female students tended to take up much less space and often had their hands on or in front of their necks or faces. They also seemed to be much less confident in the classroom and less engaged in discussion. She wondered whether there might be a relationship between posture, confidence, and performance in the classroom and elsewhere.

In one of a series of studies, she asked subjects to stand or sit for two minutes in one of two types of poses. Half the group took a "power pose," taking up large amounts of space, sitting with feet up on a desk or standing with arms wide and head up. The second group sat in a "powerless pose," which is, as you can imagine, almost the opposite. This group was instructed to take up as little space as possible, to sit or stand with legs crossed, arms crossed, and the neck or face partially or fully covered by a hand.

The results showed that body posture has a dramatic impact on body chemistry and on feelings of power. After each participant held power or powerless poses for two minutes, they were asked to evaluate their sense of power. They also engaged in an activity that measured their openness to risk. Additionally, approximately 20 minutes after the poses the participants gave a saliva sample that was compared to pre-experiment levels.

Cuddy found that the participants who had been in a power pose had dramatic increases in testosterone, a hormone associated with confidence, and decreases in cortisol, a hormone associated with stress. The participants who had been in the powerless pose had the opposite results. Their cortisol levels rocketed, demonstrating an increase in stress, while their testosterone dramatically reduced. Additionally, the Power Pose group reported much higher internal feelings of power than the other group and were more willing to take risks. The Powerless Pose group reported low levels of personal power and were more likely to be risk avoidant.

These studies reflect the science behind the exercise that you just did. Moving your body differently each time accessed a different neural network, and that neural network was then reacting inside your body and changing your biochemistry. You can now see that as you change your posture and your gestures, you change your brain and your entire system. Confidence is accessible, much more accessible than it may sometimes feel. It's simply a move, gesture, or posture change away.

In another study Cuddy discovered that the benefits extend to performance as well. In this study the subjects, after their poses, were evaluated on their performance of a brief presentation, as if they were in a job interview. The Power Pose subjects performed significantly better, demonstrating that the benefits of body posture show up in real world activities.

An Israeli researcher has taken these studies even further. Tal Shafir, at the University of Haifa in Israel, was intrigued by Cuddy's studies. She wondered if Cuddy's results with posture could be extended to dynamic movements, such as dance. She conjectured that dynamic movements would have even more measurable impact on the brain than just holding certain poses. She discovered that when people were instructed to move in certain dance steps, they then reported exactly similar emotions to other participants, without having been given instructions regarding how they should expect to feel.. After conducting her experiments, Shafir discovered that she could give people certain dance steps that would lead them to report feeling happy, feeling sad, or feeling angry, just through the movements themselves.

The results of Shafir's studies will be no surprise to you if you have ever done a "happy dance." You may have noticed that although you may only do your happy dance when you already feel happy, the dance itself increases the emotions. You may be reminded of an earlier story, when I mentioned that one of my employees was perceptive enough to observe that I skipped most often not when I already felt happy, but when I wanted to feel happy. Your posture and movements like dancing can be used in exactly the same way.

Posing Throughout Your Day

You can use your new knowledge of the body's influence on mood in two different ways. First, you now realize that your posture and gestures can be used as an INTERRUPT! step to break up moments of worry, stress, or anxiety. When you use your FIND! strategies to make yourself aware of your internal sensory channels you can also pay attention to your posture and gestures. You can ask yourself, "How was I just standing and gesturing? Did that contribute to my feelings of worry, stress, or anxiety?" You can then move into a "Power Pose," and take a stance of triumph or achievement as if you have just won a championship. You will find that this will interrupt unproductive worry and stress, reduce or eliminate anxiety, and help you feel ready to take action!

Second, you can use this strategy proactively on a daily basis. It is easy to find times to adopt a Power Pose or to dance around the room. You can make this a habit by linking it to other habits. I have a habit of making smoothies every morning. The cycle for the blender is 23 seconds, and I run it three times while I am making a smoothie. I keep one hand on the blender top during each cycle, and put my free hand into the air in a triumphant position. I find that a smile immediately bursts out on my face. This habit gives me just over a minute of a Power Pose every day to counteract any times of stress. I begin my day prepared to respond with confident action.

Take a moment to identify a time in your day when you could regularly adopt a Power Pose. Prepare yourself to INTERRUPT! worry, stress, and anxiety and build up habits that support your success and achievement. Write that time down on this page and commit to making it a part of your daily rituals. In no time, you will reap the rewards of the power wired deeply into your body.

CHAPTER FOURTEEN

POWER MOVES

You now understand the effectiveness of power poses, skipping, and dancing to interrupt your mood and your habits of worry, stress, and anxiety. The next step is to harness that power—in a form that you can use to rapidly break out of moments of stress and helplessness—so that you always have access to feelings of confidence and personal power. And the more the better!

We have seen how the movements of skipping are often connected into a neural network of feelings of joy and happiness. Most people have only skipped at times in their lives when they have felt joyful and happy; therefore, the neurons fired together and wired together.

Similarly, there are dynamic movements and postures that are likely already wired in your brain with feelings of power and confidence. Just engaging in one of these dynamic movements or postures at times of worry and stress will decrease the power of your negative emotions.

You can intensify the power of those movements and postures by strengthening the neurological wiring that connects them to the emotions of strength, power, and confidence. You will do that by remembering times when you had those emotions—vividly recalling the details of the experience and the emotions while now standing and moving in the postures and movements of power. In other words, you will intentionally fire off the neurons of the emotions by remembering them vividly, while also firing off the neurons of the movements and postures. In the simplest of terms, you will remember good times while standing tall and moving big. This allows you to exponentially strengthen pre-existing neural networks. The result is what I call a "Power Move." (This language is adopted from Tony Robbins, who has taught millions of people to use such movements while breaking through their limiting beliefs and walking across hot coals. An experience like that further reinforces the neural networks.)

A Power Move is an incredibly effective technique to very quickly banish moments of anxiety, in particular when the anxiety is associated with helplessness or hopelessness. In a moment, you will learn to develop a power move for yourself. One of my clients, who was dealing with a very anxious situation at work, had a breakthrough moment the day after she had learned her first Power Move. She was walking across the parking lot toward a meeting that was going to have a significant impact on her future with her company, and she noticed that she was feeling anxious and even fearful. She immediately engaged in her Power Move before she walked into the room. Afterwards, the people in attendance commented on the aura of confidence and power that she exhibited, not knowing that moments before–before the Power Move–she had actually been shaking in fear.

There are two steps to developing a powerful Power Move. The first is to use a physical movement that already feels strong and powerful to you. Many people use movements associated with martial arts, such as chopping motions or motions of hitting the chest and then thrusting their arms outward. Take a moment to stand up and do a movement that feels particularly powerful for you. It can be almost any movement, so long as it feels powerful. Trust your instinct. The right move is waiting for you right now, so give it a shot. You'll notice that from just this one movement you may feel better than you had the moment before. You can use just a simple movement like this as an INTERRUPT! technique in moments of worry, anxiety and stress.

Wiring the Power Move

To create a Power Move that will access your full sense of confidence, strength and power in any moment, you will now take this movement and you will wire it into a neural network connected with your strongest and most powerful memories of confidence and power. You can do this rapidly by first remembering a specific time in your life when you felt powerful, confident and strong. Do this now, while you are reading these words.

Can you remember a time when you felt powerful, confident, and strong? Can you remember a specific time? Identify a specific time and the emotion associated with it. Take a moment, go inside, and cast your mind back to that specific particular moment, feeling those sensations rushing back to you now.

To make the process even stronger, imagine floating up out of your body in this moment and floating back into that moment. See whatever you saw in that moment. Hear anything you might have heard and feel those feelings of strength, power and confidence. Good.

Imagine the feelings as an electrical current rushing through your body. As that electrical current becomes stronger, and as that feeling of power in your body moves towards a peak, make the movement that you made a moment ago! To make it even more powerful, you can shout "YES" as you do so. You can make that gesture and say "YES" and feel that sense of power. The more intensity you put into this, the more powerful it will be.

Now, stand again in a confident powerful posture and think of another time in your life when you felt strong and powerful and confident. Repeat the process, remembering to fully put yourself into that moment now and to call up those memories as if they are happening to you in this moment. As the feelings get strong within you, make your Power Move. Do it again, even more intensely.

Good. Keep going. Remember three to five times in your life when you felt powerful, confident, strong, or some combination of those emotions. Take yourself through the process with each memory, making sure to use the same Power Move each time.

If you have only been reading this section, and not doing the exercise, stop here. Go back to the top and create your own Power Move before you go any further. But first, notice that even just thinking about these events and imagining yourself making this move can bring up very strong emotions of power within you now, and with those feelings present, go ahead and let yourself do this exercise. (To see me demonstrate the creation of a Power Move go to the companion website at www.unworriedbrain.com. I can guide you along as you develop your own!)

Testing Your Power Move

Good work. Now you are in a position to test the strength of your Power Move. Take a moment and get a glass of water. Stretch as high as you can and then bend over at the waist so you touch your toes. If you can't touch them, just reach as far as you comfortably can. Take three deep breaths, mindfully noticing the movement of the air in and out of your body. You are separating yourself from the previous exercise for a moment, activating more neutral neural networks in your brain.

Now, set the book down, stand up, and make your Power Move. Go ahead! Do it now! Shout "YES!" as you do it!

This was a test of the power of your Power Move. If you immediately felt a surge of confidence, strength, and power, then you have successfully created a Power Move. Go ahead and celebrate your success! After you celebrate, make your Power Move again! This will allow you to start wiring in feelings of celebration and triumph into the same neural network as your Power Move.

If you didn't feel as much confidence, strength, and power as you would like, then celebrate the awareness of it! With that feeling of celebration as motivation, you can go back through the above exercise to strengthen the neural network. Remember to engage in high levels of emotional intensity in order to have each repetition be as effective as possible. Be playful as well. Let your fun-loving inner Super Hero come out and play!

Congratulations! You now have a Power Move. This strategy is a particularly effective way to interrupt feelings of worry or anxiety that, in the past, left you feeling helpless or hopeless. Your Power Move can activate the feelings that you need to be able to take action in moments of fear or doubt. By using your Power Move, you can put yourself in a strong, confident position to act. You now have another way to INTERRUPT! the old habits of worry, stress, and anxiety.

CHAPTER FIFTEEN

GOING FROM "OVERWHELMED" TO "FREE"

Are you having fun with the INTERRUPT! step? In the last few chapters, you've learned impactful strategies to use your physical body to affect your emotions, changing and interrupting moments of stress, worry, or anxiety. You've learned that skipping, or even imagining skipping, can bring up feelings of joy or happiness. You've learned that standing in "Power Poses" can change your body chemistry in a way that will support confidence, and that by developing a "Power Move" you can call up feelings of power that will interrupt and override any negative emotions.

Now it is time to really have some fun and unleash the power of the connection between your body and your emotions. The final strategy of INTERRUPT! will take you a step further than the previous strategies. You will notice that it not only interrupts an emotion, but also provides you with a replacement emotion after the interruption. It will lead you from the INTERRUPT! step into the REPLACE! step.

This exercise, which I call "Overwhelm to Free," is drawn from Neuro-linguistic Programming. It uses the basic brain principle that "neurons that fire together wire together." It uses dynamic **motion** and **emotion** to rewire your brain so that the neural network of feeling stressed and overwhelmed is linked to the neural network of feeling happy and free. It does this by conditioning the postures of each emotion together. In other words, it "teaches" your brain that anytime it senses you moving into the posture of overwhelm to immediately follow that with the posture of feeling free. It's simpler than it might sound. All you need to do is repeatedly, with high emotional intensity, perform the two postures with a small break between each repetition.

The Path to "Free!"

Read through the next paragraph and then follow the instructions to complete the exercise. Have fun with it!

The first step is to put yourself into an almost fetal position, leaning forward in a chair with your elbows resting on your knees and your face in your hands. You will notice almost immediately that feelings or memories of overwhelm come up quite easily in this physical posture. Stay in the posture and feelings for only two or three seconds. Then leap to your feet, throwing your arms up, taking a posture of triumph and success with your hands and fists over your head, and scream out the word "FREE!!!" Remember that the higher the emotional intensity, the greater the result. So be playful, have fun, let your neighbors hear, and move with gusto.

Go ahead! Do one repetition of this and then read the next paragraph.

Have you felt the powerful impact of this exercise? If you didn't do it, now's your chance!

What did you notice? Were you able to engage the feelings of overwhelm just for a moment and then rapidly shift those emotions as you took your triumphant pose? (To see me demonstrate the Overwhelm to Free strategy go to the companion website at www.unworriedbrain.com. Watch me get free, free, free!)

You are teaching your brain not only to connect these two postures and emotions, but to connect them in a sequence so that the moments of overwhelm lead you to both the posture and the feelings of freedom. Now if you're really ready to improve your life, which I know you are, then do several repetitions of this. Try for 5, 10, 15, 20. If you're feeling really bravely committed to yourself and achievement, do 50! It's just like working out. It can take will power at first. Then once you've started, it feels great.

Remember one thing as you go ahead and do a series of these now. After each repetition, take a moment to "shake off" the good feelings before returning to the position of overwhelm. Simply shake your body for a few seconds after you complete one repetition, then dive back into the next. You want your brain to make the connection only in one direction, going from overwhelm to empowerment and freedom.

Now go have fun with this. And make sure you feel free, free, free before you move on to the next section!

SECTION FOUR

REPLACE!

CHAPTER SIXTEEN

INTRODUCING THE REPLACE! STEP

Congratulations on becoming an interrupting superhero! You now have one of the most socially annoying powers known to humans. You can interrupt with the best of them.

More importantly, you can interrupt your habits. You have accumulated a Thought Cavalry, a Power Move, easy access to feeling free anytime you want, and lots of other powerful INTERRUPT! tools. Now that you have some momentum, you can take a look at where you are in your progress.

At this point you should have a degree of comfort with the FIND! step. By consistently practicing the Celebrate Awareness strategy, you have been teaching your brain to bring the moments of worry, stress, and anxiety to consciousness so you can respond to them with action. You can immediately ask yourself, "How did I just create that emotion?

What was I visualizing, imagining, remembering, or picturing? What was I saying to myself, and how? What sensations or feelings was I focusing on, and what was I labeling them?"

You also now realize how those questions lead to the INTERRUPT! process, and you have a series of strategies for interrupting your old habits. You have already begun to interrupt certain moments of stress, worry, and anxiety with playfulness, with joy, and with brand new physical experiences. In doing so, you've already started to disrupt the fixed pattern of your old habits. They are now less stable, creating an opening for brand new thoughts, emotions, and behaviors.

This is a key time. Your old habits are shaking in their metaphorical boots, shuddering at the edge of a cliff, worried that you may jump out and INTERRUPT! them at any moment. You are no longer the same habit zombie you once were. You are less unconscious, less habitual, and less certain.

But here's a news flash: this can't last.

Why? As we've said, your brain will not allow a vacuum. Your brain will always step in to replace an old habit with something new, something that can be on "zombie-pilot." If the momentum of the habits of worry, stress, and anxiety are strong enough, and there isn't anything else that is stronger, then your brain will go back to the negative feelings or other problematic habits. As you learned in the brain principles chapter, the brain circuits of old habits never completely go away. That's why the REPLACE! phase is so important. This is where you take control of intentionally creating your new experience. This is where you gain access to new feelings, new thoughts, and new behaviors that will begin to structure your new, empowering habits.

You may have noticed that you have already begun to have new feelings and thoughts. The INTERRUPT! strategies bring these with them as they disrupt the worry, stress, and anxiety. All you have to do is support and sustain them after each instance of skipping, Power Moves, Thought Cavalry, etc. Inside each of these strategies is a seamless movement from INTERRUPT! to REPLACE!

For long term sustainability, however, it is important to REPLACE! other habits that have maintained and supported the worry, stress, and anxiety. That is the focus of the chapters inside the REPLACE! step. Specifically, you will learn to REPLACE! habits of language, metaphor, focus, and mindless behavior. Each new replacement will make it easier for you to habituate new, positive habits of calm, confident action. That final habituation will be covered in the EXERCISE! step.

In these next four chapters, you will learn some of my favorite strategies. You will learn to become dramatically more productive. You will be introduced to one of the most heavily-researched methods to strengthen your brain. You will learn to overcome the invisible traps buried deep within your metaphors. And you will be surprised to find out that your high school English teacher really was right—your language matters.

CHAPTER SEVENTEEN

USING YOUR BRAIN FOR PRODUCTIVITY

This chapter will focus on REPLACE! strategies for greater productivity. You might be saying, "Finally!" It's true that many instances of worry, stress, and anxiety are really intended to make you more productive, to get you working harder and achieving more. Unfortunately that doesn't work. So what does? Using your new knowledge of the brain to implement REPLACE! strategies that not only break the old habits, but also improve your productivity and allow you to achieve at a higher level. Woohoo!

That's the focus of this section: "Gettin' it done!" You will learn how to combine a brain-based time management strategy with a brain-based focus strategy to exponentially improve your productivity. You get better focus in less time for more results.

First, think for a moment about being focused and productive... Aren't there times when it isn't easy to stay on task, even when you have interrupted any unproductive worry and stress? You might think that it would be simple at that point to just be productive. After all, you have interrupted the old habits of stress and worry, overcoming the obstacle, and the path to accomplish and achieve should now be ahead of you. You have used productive worry to direct your attention to what needs to happen, and you have harnessed the strength of the stress response to have all your resources behind you. You are ready to direct this energy into constructive action. Shouldn't it all be easy now to progress? But it's not.

To understand why it's often not so easy to focus and be productive, think for a moment about the early historical context of worry and stress. If worry and stress play the role of activating action, what kind of actions did they usually activate in the early days of humankind? Answer this for yourself before you read on.

If a 'caveman' running from a wild animal immediately came to mind, then you are in the right neighborhood. In early human history, people felt stress in response to life-threatening situations.

The caveman's productive worry brought his attention to danger signals in the environment. It combined with the stress response to generate a heightened awareness and then a full-out sprint to the safety of the cave. In that context, survival could be considered the height of productivity! Accordingly, in early human history the most appropriate actions in response to productive worry and stress were physical actions like fleeing or bracing for an attack.

Your present context is probably quite different. Even though your brain is hardwired for the sprint to the cave, many of the actions that will best address the circumstances of your worry and stress probably take place at a desk, working on a computer, talking on the phone, or in direct conversation—things not inherently wired into the fight or flight response. To achieve and be successful these days, you have to be self-directed and stay focused for hours on end.

Unfortunately, the most difficult time for you to focus is probably when you are on a computer or other device, reading, writing, and otherwise processing information. This then leads to greater stress, which can then lead to anxiety and less productivity, which in turn leads to greater stress and worry. Despite the intensity of stress or need to take action, many people have developed bad habits of "multi-tasking" and of distraction, both of which undermine the most productive uses of stress and worry.

"Multitasking" –Does it Work?

Research on the brain has shown that what we call "multitasking" is better referred to as "switch tasking." Rather than divide its focus between several tasks simultaneously, the brain actually switches rapidly between them. The brain does this so quickly that it feels like we're focusing on more than one thing at a time, but we are not. More importantly, there is actually a loss of energy, of efficiency, every single time we switch back and forth. The brain has to readjust its focus and get back into 'full gear' every time it switches. These seemingly small losses of efficiency add up over time, causing us to underperform and burnout, which in turn causes more stress, worry, and anxiety.

Studies have also surprisingly shown that frequent multi-taskers do not get better at it—they get worse![14] Heavy media multi-taskers were actually poorer at returning their focus after switching, and processed less information in all of the tasks. And yes, that is a bad thing.

Multi-tasking presents a problem, but full-blown distraction is even more destructive to the actions we need to take to reduce worry and stress. Distraction takes us completely away from what needs our attention. Worse yet, it is often a habit of avoidance or procrastination. With both habits—habits of multitasking and habits of distraction—we make it that much harder to release worry, anxiety, and stress. Therefore, to fully put unproductive worry and stress behind you it is important to have strategies to protect you against these temptations.

In this section, we will focus on two particular REPLACE! strategies that will allow you to counteract and resist the habits of distraction and multitasking. You will notice how each of them implements the full FIRE! process. For extra credit, challenge yourself to identify the elements of FIND! and INTERRUPT! inside of these strategies.

Recall the story of Jessica from the introduction story. In her anxiety and distress, she forced herself to stay at her desk for hours even when she was unproductive and unhappy. She felt guilty about any break, yet she was constantly distracted by her emotions while she was "working" at her desk. Just working more wasn't really working, to say the least.

She desperately needed this first strategy, a strategy of time management. You may need it, too. In your desire to take actions to reduce your worry and stress, you may very well overestimate the amount of time that you can stay focused on any task. It's not uncommon for some people to put off an activity until the last moment and then attempt to spend hours in a row working on it. The human brain is not well-equipped for that amount of dedicated focus.

In fact, studies on attention support the notion that the brain functions best in interval formats, that is cycles of "on" and "off," cycles of focus and rest. You may have heard about the effectiveness of intervals in fitness training and the way in which intense periods of exercise followed by rest allow for greater fitness gains than longer, extended periods of exercise. The same is true for focus. Briefer, dedicated periods of focus followed by equally dedicated periods of rest, and/or intentional distraction, are much more effective than attempted periods of long and sustained focus.

You need to incorporate "interval training" into your daily work schedule. Ideally, you will stay focused on one topic for no more than 30-50 minutes in a stretch. The 30-50 minute interval will then be immediately followed by a period of intentional distraction. The rest or distraction period should engage in a very different use of the body and brain. It should also be in a different physical location than where you worked. In other words, when you focus, focus no more than 30 or 50 minutes in a row. Then get up, move your body, use different brain functions, and change your location.

It may not be easy to imagine taking a break every 30-50 minutes, especially if your previous habits of stress and worry have put you in a situation where you need to be extremely productive on short notice. This was Jessica's situation; she was studying 14-16 hours a day and still not getting her work done. I suggested to her that she not only take regular breaks, but that she engage in the most restricted form of interval focus, spending the day alternating between 30 minutes of focus and 15 minute breaks. She was initially astonished and almost indignant at this suggestion. She naturally believed that if she couldn't get her work done in 14-16 hours a day, it would be absurd to think that she could get it done by taking a full third of that time off to rest and distract herself!

Jessica was committed, however, to releasing her unhealthy habits of worry, stress, and anxiety. She gave herself permission to experiment with this method. Within a week, she was convinced. In fact, she found that by implementing the 30/15 strategy along with the Shiny Penny Defense strategy (covered below), she was able to stay fully focused for those 30-minute blocks. She realized how little of her previous study time had been at full focus. She actually became so much more productive that her entire study time, including the 15-minute breaks, was reduced by a third. The beneficial side effect for her, which you might also experience, was that she had more time left over to sleep and rejuvenate, which helped her to stay focused day after day.

To Make This Work, Follow the Instructions Carefully

It is helpful to be very specific on the implementation of this strategy, and to highlight the methods to make it a habit. Your first step as you experiment with this process is to use an alarm, or even better, your smartphone, to track the time periods. Set a 30-minute timer the moment you sit down. You will then stay focused during those 30 minutes with the help of the next strategy you will learn. When the timer goes off, immediately set another timer for the 15-minute break. Stop yourself exactly where you are, even if you feel like you're still in the flow or you have more ideas or more actions to take. The more often you do this, the more you learn to trust the pattern.

The activities during the break should be as different as possible from whatever you are doing during your focus period. For example, if you are sitting still at your desk for 30 minutes, you can take your break with brief periods of exercise, bouncing on a rebounder or doing pushups. If you know how, you can juggle or play a musical instrument, clean or take a walk. (I strongly recommend the juggling or playing an instrument, because these activate very different brain processes from traditional mental focus.)

If you are going to check your email or Facebook, do so in a different location than where you were working. If you are a social person but have to focus during solitary time at your desk, use your break time to socialize and connect. You will feel more energized when you return.

Who Uses This?

You may be interested to know that I have used the 30/15 strategy regularly throughout the time of writing this book. The largest intervals I have allowed myself were structured 50/10, that is, 50 minutes of focus followed by a fully dedicated 10 minutes of break. I recommend you stay with the 30/15 arrangement until you are able to consistently remain focused for 30 minute intervals. Then you can slowly expand to 40. Then 50. Only after that should you reduce the break time.

Some of my favorite things to do during that break are to bounce on my rebounder and to juggle. The juggling has an additional benefit because it engages the body and actually activates both sides of the brain as well. I highly recommend it, especially because it is just as effective if you do it poorly or if you do it well. (Go to the companion website at www.unworriedbrain.com for a demonstration of how to juggle poorly and enjoy it. I have a great time with it.)

You can practice this strategy, and the next one, even while reading this book. Take a moment now and set a timer for 30 minutes. Commit yourself during this time to stay fully focused and engaged. Promise yourself that you will take a break at the end of the time and then return with new energy and renewed commitment. Set the timer now.

The next strategy is designed to assist you during your 30 minutes of focus. By understanding the concepts of the interval and how these work with your brain, you're already on your way to staying more focused and combatting distraction. Just knowing that you will get a break can give you the permission necessary to stay focused longer. You can maintain that focus even longer, and be even more productive, if you more fully take advantage of your understanding of the brain.

Did you set your timer yet? Set it for 30 minutes in order to get the most out of the next strategy.

From Shoes to Pennies

You have already been introduced to one of the most powerful and most playful strategies available to remind your brain to stay focused. Do you remember the shoe? It's probably on your desk right now, right? If not, at least it's in your mind every time you see a shoe on one of these pages. The shoe strategy relies on the brain's ability to rapidly give meaning to a new stimulus in the environment. You can engage that strategy with even more sophistication through what I call the "Shiny Penny Defense." Have you ever heard of the 'shiny penny' metaphor, the idea that everyone has the capacity to become instantly distracted by something shiny? Well, this is your time to use a stack of shiny pennies to never be distracted by a 'shiny penny' again.

Get yourself ten pennies (the shinier the better). Then put them on your desk at the beginning of a 30-minute focus interval. If you have easy access to ten pennies, go and get them now and put them on your desk. As long as the pennies are in your visual field, and you have committed yourself to staying focused during this time by putting the pennies on your desk, then your brain will automatically shift its awareness to the pennies at any moments of distraction. In this way, the stack of pennies will function like the shoe; it is a novel stimulus that reminds you of your commitment to stay on task.

The pennies can be used with more subtlety than the shoe, though. By placing the pennies on your desk, your brain associates the act of staying focused with the act of noticing the pennies. Therefore, the simple presence of the pennies will bring to awareness any moment of distraction. Once aware, you then have a choice about how to act. You can choose to redirect your attention and go back to work. Or not. Either way, it is a fully conscious decision.

The Shiny Penny Defense strategy doesn't require that you choose to stay focused every time you feel the pull of distraction, although that is the goal. It simply commits you to acknowledging that your moment of distraction is intentional—is a choice. Each time you choose to break from your task, you will move a penny off the stack. At the end of your 30 minute interval of focus, count how many pennies you moved from the stack. The number will show you how many times you've allowed yourself to be distracted.

By keeping track in this way, you make it possible to improve. Each time you end a session, you know better how much effort you need to stay focused. Additionally, if you realize that you moved a lot of pennies, you may need to wonder whether the task is really your highest priority in the moment. You should only use the penny stack for tasks that you are committed to focusing on. Otherwise it is better to complete the higher priorities first. And when you return to work, the penny stacks will be there, reminding you to recommit to your focus, allowing you to get better at staying on task.

Here's Another Possibility - Accept the Challenge!

On the other hand, you can harness your drive and competitive nature to go head to head with the distraction. You may find your mind wandering, then you see the pennies and realize that you have a choice: give into idle distraction or go inside and call up that competitive spirit. You might say to yourself, for example, "Really? I'm going to allow myself to be distracted when there are only 12 more minutes? I can't wait 12 little minutes before I check my phone? Are you kidding me? Bring it on!" The more fervor and commitment you get in your inner voice at that time, the more you sit in this bulldog state, the more likely you are to pull up your power and energy so you can return to your task. Each time you choose to stay focused, you will feel more power and you will train your brain to stay focused. And you will have defeated distraction! Hah!

At the end of each one of those intervals, you know what to do, right? Celebrate!

Celebrate as hard as you can. Reward yourself for staying focused. Celebration, of course, wires in the new habit of focus that will then allow you to support only the productive uses of worry and stress. Celebration, of course, rewards you for your champion spirit and commitment to living a productive and anxiety-free life. And celebration, of course, is its own reward.

Hey, I just finished this chapter. Excuse me while I go celebrate! Of course!

CHAPTER EIGHTEEN

REPLACE! YOUR LANGUAGE

The next strategies in the REPLACE! step are language strategies, focusing on how you use language throughout your life. The language that you use is important because it directly impacts your brain. In a fascinating set of studies, it has been shown that language that is being used metaphorically or as a figure of speech activates the part of the brain that would be literally associated with the connotations and denotations associated with the words.[15]

For example, if I were to ask you now to consider whether you would ever be willing to run for office, and we were able to observe your brain functioning while you read the sentence, we would see activation in the part of your brain, the motor cortex, that is associated with physical movement. You may not have thought that this use of the word "run" could ever be thought to be anything but metaphorical, that "run for office" has nothing at all to do with physical activity of running, yet your brain experiences it differently.

This is an illustration of how your word choice directly accesses and affects your brain. Similarly, the word choices you have become habituated to using in your habits of worry, stress, and anxiety are linked and connected with the maintenance and continuation of those emotions. To change the emotions you must change the language.

Your Brain 'Listens' to your Language

One of the primary ways in which language affects you, in particular with habits of emotion, is through language of your identity. Just like everyone else in the world, you use language to make claims about who you are, or what kind of person you are, or what you do in life. These are statements that often start with or use "I am," or "I am the kind of person who. . . " phrases. We are all familiar with this, but what you may not have known until now is that these statements are hugely impactful because they self-perpetuate and self-reinforce.

Here's why: these identity statements are used by your brain to prioritize the information that should receive focus. As you will recall, there is always more information being processed by your brain than can be accessed consciously at any one time. Therefore, your brain is constantly having to prioritize information to determine what is important enough to deserve attention. Your brain is also a self-organizing system—that is, information and frameworks that have previously been learned are used to filter and categorize new information and experiences.

The result is that if you describe yourself as an anxious person, you instruct your brain to prioritize information that could possibly be categorized as "anxiety provoking." Situations that could lead to dangerous circumstances are given a higher priority. If you describe yourself as a "confident person," you are instead instructing your brain to prioritize information or situations that allow you to act confidently. Simply put, once you make an identity claim, your brain seeks evidence to prove your assertion.

So, what should you do? Should you claim to feel calm and confident even when you don't? Maybe, and maybe not. Affirmations are not always an easy step when you have had a longtime habit of worry, stress, and anxiety. You may not yet be ready to claim for yourself that you are a competent person, a calm person, or even a happy person. Making these claims might stir in you a feeling of dissonance, or incongruence, because they are currently at odds with your most recent identity. You may need to accept this for the time being.

There is, however, a preliminary step you can take to prepare yourself to adopt such self identity claims. You can do this by using your language in a way that calls to attention, prioritizes, or filters information that you want your brain to focus on. You can use your language to direct your brain's unconscious filters and focus.

The Presents of Present Tense Strategy

The "Presents of Present Tense" is a play on words, inviting you to give yourself a present (a gift) of a more empowering use of your present-tense language. Present-tense language is critically important because it is the most common language used to create identity statements. When you think of how you commonly use present-tense language, you can realize that it is used for more than simply referring to the present.

If I say, "I am an anxious person," I may say that even in a moment when I am not feeling anxious. I'm using present tense language to refer to moments from my past and express the expectation that my future will be similar. Thus, I am making a claim about my identity. As we just observed, this is an unconscious message to my brain to prioritize information that will support that statement.

The Presents of Present Tense strategy is a method for diminishing undesirable characteristics from your identity. To start eliminating any emotion or behavior that you do not wish to continue in the future, even if you believe that it has been true of you up to this point, simply use past-tense constructions. Using the past tense is a more accurate description of what you know to be true about the world. You only know about your past behavior and emotions.

For example, instead of saying, "I worry," which implies that this is a part of your identity and will be true in the future as well, you might say instead, "I worried yesterday." You could also say, "I have worried recently," or even "I used to worry." If that last statement does not feel congruent for you, you could make it both more playful and more accurate by saying, "I used to worry, even as recently as earlier today." This may bring a smile to your face, and it will also make your brain more likely to change in future circumstances. In other words, a statement like that does not affect prioritization, and therefore it will help you be more open to positive change.

Instead of saying, "I get so anxious," or "I'm an anxious person," just say, "I've gotten anxious in the past," or "I often got anxious before." It's really more accurate since you don't know what you will do in the future. Use this for any emotion or behavior that hasn't served you well.

This is different from positive thinking or affirmations. You are not making new and optimistic claims about how you will be in the future, but instead you are simply reducing the negative impact of your past view of yourself. This prevents that past view, expressed in your identity statements, from creating a self-fulfilling prophecy.

Only use present-tense language for descriptions that you wish to continue to be true in the future. For example, you might say, "I am patient," or "I am a good learner," if you believe it's true of you. These are positive examples of present-tense language that are about more than just the present. These are examples that build and strengthen desirable aspects of the person you have been, who you currently are, and who you want to be in the future.

It is true that there are some examples of present-tense language that are obviously just about the present—about this moment. I may use an "I am" statement to give you information about my present circumstances. I may say, for example, "I am sitting in this chair." You can continue to say things like that. It is very important to distinguish that from the present-tense language of identity statements, which are actually less focused on the present than on the past, and on an expectation or belief that the future will be the same as the past. Put negative identity statements in the past every time you notice them.

Go ahead and use this strategy now, by thinking of some of the present tense claims you have made about yourself in the past regarding your identity as someone who was worried, stressed, or anxious. Repeat that statement, but in the past tense instead. Notice how it feels.

Then continue the practice in real time, any time you may catch yourself making such a first-person statement. Immediately notice it, celebrate your awareness for a moment, and then repeat the statement in the past tense. It might sound like this: "I am a really anxious person. Oh, what I meant to say was, I used to be an anxious person, even right up to today." Go ahead and have a little fun with it. Recognize that this replacement strategy is a powerful step in moving your experience to a positive cycle and away from habits of worry, stress, and anxiety.

Channeling Your Inner Athlete - The Third Person Language Strategy

Have you ever noticed how often athletes talk about themselves in the third person? Instead of saying "I," they will use their name, or say "he" or "she." When Floyd Mayweather was asked about the best thing about boxing, he said, "The fans. Because without the fans Floyd Mayweather wouldn't be who he is." When LeBron James announced his decision to join the Miami Heat, he said, ""I wanted to do what was best, you know, for LeBron James, and what LeBron James was gonna do to make him happy."

It has become such a joke that Esquire Magazine ran a column on it with the subtitle "Esquire Magazine is going to discuss the proper use of the third person, and Esquire Magazine doesn't think you're going to have a problem with that."

The third-person language used by the athletes creates a distance between them and their statements. That can make them seem bigger than life and creates the impression that their statements are more than just an expression of their opinions; they are saying, 'This isn't about me.'

Indeed! They have hit on something very important, something that can help you with feelings of anxiety. This language strategy was researched recently in the field of social anxiety.[16] Researchers found that their subjects, anxious about an upcoming event, could reduce that anxiety dramatically just by talking about it in the third person!

How might that work? The researchers discovered that individuals who are feeling anxious, and who in particular are feeling anxious about an upcoming event, very often will talk to themselves and others about their feelings regarding the event. As they do so, the self talk or conversations increase the feelings of anxiety. The more they talk or think about the anxiety-producing event, the more anxious they become.

This anxiety acceleration process can be interrupted and greatly reduced by simply changing the language of the self talk or conversations. Move from the normal first-person structure of using "I," and instead use a third-person structure, which would use "he" or "she" and your name.

I can use myself as an example. In my case, it would be moving away from saying, "I am really worried about my speaking engagement tomorrow." Instead, I might say, "Brad is really worried about his speaking engagement tomorrow." I would then continue to talk about myself in the third person. "Here's what Brad is feeling."

This is a startlingly powerful process. Experiment with it yourself even as you're reading these words. Think about an event that is coming up in your near future. This should be an event that you have been worrying about. Begin to talk about yourself, but use the third person. If you don't find this to be simple immediately effective, you can take a playful approach to it and think about it as channeling your inner "LeBron James."

As you talk in third person about this upcoming event, you will notice yourself feeling more playful and less worried. You will find it easier to move yourself to more empowering questions, such as, "What has [your name here] been able to do in similar circumstances?'" Or, "What are the positive elements of this situation?'" In the past, you may have found it difficult to do this when you were caught up in the anxiety. Using the third person strategy releases you from the intensity of the emotion, and you can then more naturally find solutions. You can 'coach' yourself.

It is certainly easier for me, for example, to follow an internal thought of "Brad is feeling worried about an upcoming event," with a leading question such as, "What has Brad done in the past that has helped him with this?" Then I might ask myself, "How might Brad begin to feel better right now about this situation?" As I answer that question, I will continue to talk about "Brad" rather than using "I." It is easier than you might think for me to answer those questions by listing the resources that "Brad" has used in the past and to feel the positive emotions and resourcefulness that this generates.

As you use this strategy, you will find that the emotional intensity of the worry, stress, or anxiety will diminish. You now have a sufficient understanding of the workings of the brain to recognize how this is happening. By speaking in the third person, you are shifting the neural network. You are accessing a different set of wiring. This different set of wiring—talking about other people in the third person—is associated with much less emotion. You are probably like most people and have tended to take your own experiences more seriously, or with more intense emotion, than the experiences of others. You are "hacking" into that wiring by using the third person language, even though the conversation is still really about you. You are obtaining sufficient emotional distance to be able to access your resources.

This is a powerful replacement process—one that I use regularly. Perhaps I should say instead, "Brad continues to use this regularly, whenever he needs it." Go ahead and join Brad in this extremely powerful process and have some fun with it. He certainly does!

CHAPTER NINETEEN

MINDFULNESS AND MEDITATION

My body lay quiet and motionless on the surgery table. Around me the surgeons bustled and chatted as they prepared to repair my torn Achilles tendon. They made no effort to be quiet, secure in their experience of operating on countless patients under full general anesthesia. The surgeon cut into my leg and pulled out the ends of the tendon, then tied them together. The rest of my body didn't even twitch. My consciousness was far away.

As the surgeon completed his work, stitching up my leg, a phone rang in the operating room. There was a muffled conversation and then the surgeon said, "Oops."

Immediately, I responded. "Oops?" I said. "What is this, a joke?"

The surgeon jerked, startled, and several nurses laughed nervously. They had all forgotten I was not under anesthesia for the entire surgery. They had forgotten that I was in a deep meditative state instead. Even as I had put my body in a completely relaxed and unresponsive state, and as my consciousness was far away in a peaceful visualization, I had left some part of my mind to monitor the conversation, and it pulled me back in response to the surgeon's comment. "What about that 'Oops?'" I continued. "Is there something I should know?"

The surgeon reassured me that his comment had nothing to do with me, that it was a reference to the phone call regarding their next patient, who had mistakenly eaten a meal just minutes before surgery and would have to be delayed. I laughingly accepted his explanation and he went on to finish the surgery, but he was clearly no longer at ease, extremely aware of my awake state. He had not been comfortable with my insistence on using this meditative self-hypnosis state instead of general anesthesia, but he had compromised in the face of my persistence as long as I was willing for him to use a topical anesthesia where he had cut my leg. Other than the topical anesthetic, I was using only the power of my brain.

Master Meditation in a Flash

Have you heard stories like this? Have you even heard of the monks who, after years of practice, can generate so much heat while meditating that they can dry sheets soaked in freezing water? Or of other meditators who can reduce their metabolism and cut their oxygen consumption in half?[17] Even if none of this is news to you, you may think you could never meditate for the years that it might take to really make an impact—to change your brain and become more mindful.

But wait! Although it is not possible to download a program like Neo in the Matrix and become a master at meditation, let alone a master of martial arts like Neo, there is hope. Studies have shown that there are significant brain changes in as little as eight weeks with Mindfulness Based Stress Reduction (MBSR), a well known mindfulness training program.[18] These studies on changes in the brain are parallel to studies that have shown that a similar timeframe of meditation can show significant life results—reductions in anxiety and increases in empathy and in life satisfaction.

I didn't set out on the path of meditation and self-hypnosis in order to experience surgery without anesthesia. I set out just like you, in order to reduce feelings of worry, stress, and anxiety, and (in my case at least) to help others to do so. I found that clients in my clinical practice experienced rapid and sustained benefit from even as little as two to four minutes a day of MBSR or similar practices. It was more effective with longer durations, but consistent habits over very short periods still produced good results.

Many of my clients were struggling with chronic pain alongside their stress and anxiety, which led me to begin practicing a meditative trance for pain control. That led me to practice using it to replace anesthesia, first in the controlled environment of the dental chair. I thought that was the safest start because the dentist could always come through with a shot. Surprisingly, I never needed it. I was able to manage the pain from the beginning, and eventually began to be able to generate anesthetic symptoms such as numbness and difficulty talking after the dental surgery. I was shocked. I have since continued to practice many different forms of meditation.

Mindfulness meditation is a wonderful REPLACE! strategy. It can be done in response to immediate signs of stress, worry, or anxiety (like an INTERRUPT! strategy), or even better on a consistent basis. Then it begins to REPLACE! habits of mindless behavior and trains your brain to control your zombie-like habitual behavior. As I mentioned before, it is good (and inevitable) to be a habit zombie, as long as you are intentional about your habits, but it is best as a part-time affair. Although we cannot be aware and mindful every moment, our lives benefit from regular periods of simply being as aware as possible of everything around us. MBSR (and other mindfulness and meditative practices), when done consistently, make us into that contradictory self-aware zombie.

You have lots of options for introducing mindfulness and meditation into your life. Many major metropolitan areas (and some smaller ones) have MBSR programs. You can start there. You can go "bigger" and go away for a two-week silent retreat, or go "smaller" and just begin practicing daily mindfulness from a book. My favorite is *How to Train a Wild Elephant: And Other Adventures in Mindfulness* by Jan Chosen Bays.[19] It has 53 simple practices to encourage and develop daily mindfulness. The practices are perfectly "bite-sized" for daily or weekly focus. Many of them are playful, and I have incorporated some of them into regular use—such as using my left hand, a moment of gratitude at the end of a day, silly walking, and others. I highly recommend it.

In this chapter, I will offer some specific suggestions and stories from my therapy and coaching practices. These are meditative approaches, and one technology, that have been particularly helpful for specific circumstances but can be used for great effect generally as well.

Worried or Scattered? Train Your Brain With Meditation

Richard Davidson has done many of the early studies on the power of meditation and its effects on the brain. I recommend his book, *The Emotional Life of Your Brain*.[20] He has meditation suggestions for different emotional styles. I have found a specific combination to be extremely helpful for clients who have come to me with difficulty focusing, especially due to worry.

I recommend a combination of two different meditation practices—Tracking the Mind and One Pointed Concentration. These exercises are adapted from his book mentioned above. Together they train the brain to be aware of distraction and to cultivate the ability to return from the distraction. They can be a great support if you are not finding it easy to keep your focus during the focus blocks, even with the help of your stack of pennies. You can do the meditative exercises in either order, but I suggest starting with just a few minutes of each of them with an equal break in between.

One Pointed Concentration Exercise

In this exercise, you will focus your attention on a single physical object, returning your attention to it if at any time you are unable to stay focused on the object. This practice helps replace the business of a worried mind with the attention and focus needed to perform at your peak.

1. Sit in a quiet space with minimal distractions. Identify a particular small object, such as a rock, coin, or button. It is important that this be a physical, three-dimensional object.

2. Keep your eyes open and focused on the object.

3. Leave your mind quiet other than the visual focus on the object.

4. If your attention wanders, calmly and non-judgmentally bring it back to the object. While you maintain your attention on the visual focus on the object, let any additional thoughts simply pass by.

5. The key practice in this exercise is the non-judgmental return to a focus point. You are wiring your brain to be able to easily regain focus even if distracting thoughts arise.

6. Do this exercise twice a day—initially for two minutes, then five minutes. When you are

comfortable, extend it to ten minutes. Combine
it with Tracking the Mind.

Tracking the Mind Exercise

This exercise focuses on creating a "monitoring"
mechanism within your own mind, such that you
can be aware of your own thoughts and your mind's
movement from one thought to the other. You are
to allow the mind to move; your focus is on noticing
and commenting non-judgmentally on each change
of focus.

1. Sit comfortably, preferably with your back
   straight. You may have your eyes open or
   closed.
2. Start with the initial attitude of a calm and
   relaxed mind with no specific focus.
3. Lightly attend to whatever comes to mind,
   observing the thinking without further engaging
   with it. "I notice that I am now thinking about. .
   ."
4. Give your full awareness to this object of
   awareness while allowing it freedom to go or stay
   in the forefront of your consciousness. Stay
   unattached to it while observing it interestedly.
   Whatever the thought, just notice it.
5. Track your mind as it moves to another
   thought, allowing that to become the center of
   attention. Remain aware of whatever comes into
   your consciousness, observing it without
   exploring it or giving it any additional

importance except as the thought that is currently in your mind.

6. Continue the process for five minutes. If you are unable to stay fully with the process, then notice that as well, permitting that to be the center of your attention, thus resuming the process.

7. Start with two minutes twice a day, then move each set up to five minutes. Then expand to ten minutes when you are able to do five minutes comfortably. Combine it with One Pointed Concentration.

Long-Term Stress in the Body

A 70-year-old man, Ernie, came to me only one time. He was bent over, and his shoulders and neck were so hunched that it was difficult for him to look up at me. His first words were, "I've been stressed for 50 years, since I took my first job. It's got into my body now, and I hurt all the time. Is there any hope for me?"

I said, "Yes, of course. The good news is that there have been lots of moments of 'non-stress' during those 50 years and your brain remembers them, even though you don't yet. You just have to learn how to go get them and bring them into your body instead. To do that you must break the cycle of mindless stress. That starts with mindfulness."

I taught him the FIRE! process and emphasized the importance of celebrating each time he was aware of the stress in his body so that he could do something about it. Then he began to use a mindfulness strategy, Body Awareness, as both an INTERRUPT! and REPLACE! strategy. He could use the strategy while lying down for maximum impact, or he could just do it while standing or sitting if necessary. The strategies Ernie learned in this single meeting were all he would need to totally overhaul his life. As you read about this technique, you can follow along in your own body.

Body Awareness Exercise

If you are lying down or sitting, begin by noticing your feet. If you are standing up, it is easier to begin with the top of the head instead. For this written version, I will assume you are lying down or sitting. Read along slowly, pausing to allow your awareness to focus on each body part mentioned. If at any moment you notice the awareness straying, just non-judgmentally bring it back, as in the above exercise.

Notice your feet. Let your awareness sweep slowly through every muscle in your feet. Notice the relaxation level of each foot. (Note that I didn't say "the stress level" but "the relaxation level.") Is one foot more relaxed than the other, even ever so slightly? Notice which foot might be more relaxed. Allow your mind to just wonder languidly whether your other foot could become equally relaxed. Let that happen or not happen, as you let your awareness peacefully look for each sign of relaxation in your feet.

Let your awareness drift slowly up to your calves. Is either one of your calves more relaxed than the other? Notice which calf might be more relaxed and wonder whether the other calf could become equally relaxed. Let that happen or not happen, as you let your awareness peacefully look for each sign of relaxation in your calves.

Move your awareness to your knees, then your thighs, upper legs, bottom and lower back, and repeat the process, breathing slowly and giving your full, patient attention to it.

Continue through your upper body, taking separate moments particularly for your shoulders, your neck, your face, and your scalp. Remember to breathe. Remember to take it slowly and patiently.

At the end, take a moment to survey your entire body, finding signs of relaxation anywhere they may be. Thank your body for its relaxation.

You can do this process very slowly or less slowly, depending on how much time you have. When you do it less slowly, still do it peacefully and calmly.

Fast Results

As I said, I only saw Ernie once. He called me up the next day with awe in his voice. He said that later that day, after he had gone home, he had practiced his FIND! step and noticed stress in his body. He had been in a public place when he noticed it, but he let himself do a little celebration dance anyway. This made him laugh, which immediately broke his stress habit. Then he went through the body awareness process and was shocked to find that his feelings of stress and pain were cut in half immediately. He contacted me once more, months later, to report his gratitude and continued results. He felt twenty years younger, he kept saying—"Twenty years younger."

Balance Your Brain

The first time a client walks into my office I am expecting obvious signs of anxiety or distress. But it wasn't that way with one client, Katherine. She stepped in, smiling and looking confident. That's what made it worse for her. Inside, she said, she was terrified. She had felt unreasoning fear and anxiety since childhood but had learned to conceal it. When she would share her feelings with others, it was hard for them to accept the depth of the distress, because they couldn't see the signs. She had almost decided to stop seeking ways to feel better, until she realized that her young son could sense when she was anxious. He became upset whenever she was upset. That's when she became determined to find an answer.

When Katherine began researching options to help her, she found an intriguing possibility that brought her to me. She had seen online that I was providing a brain balancing technology, Brainwave Optimization™. She admitted that she was looking for a 'magic bullet,' something that would just take it all away from her. She had heard that all she had to do was sit in a chair for ten sessions and this technology would balance her brain.

Well, yes and no. I was using Brainwave Optimization™ with clients because of its exceptional capability to support the brain in its natural meditative and self-healing capacities. The technology translates brainwave activity into sounds which are fed into headphones. The brain recognizes the sounds for what they are, representations of its own activity, and it adjusts in response. It is almost as if it is 'looking' into a 'mirror,' and can use that information to balance brainwave activity that has been thrown out of balance by stress or traumatic experiences. The resulting brainwave activity is similar to that shown by experienced meditators and is experienced as increased serenity, calm, and flexibility. I have used it myself and experienced increased energy, focus, and a sense of being grounded—much as I feel after a deep meditative trance. But it is not a 'magic bullet.' Even a balanced brain benefits from knowing how to deal with future stress without falling back into bad habits.

Katharine was initially disappointed at the idea that she would have to do more than just 'listen to her brain,' but she quickly embraced the combination of the FIRE! process and the support of the Brainwave Optimization™ technology. She soon felt like she had been meditating for years, and her brainwave patterns balanced and stayed balanced. She integrated the Visual Fade strategy to break her decades-long pattern of obsessing on painful past events, and she was able to respond in new ways to previously stressful events—calling up the calm meditative state she felt during Brainwave Optimization™ as she gradually let go of her fears. After several months, she walked into my office one day, smiling and as confident looking as ever, and spun around, laughing. "Can you see what's different?" she asked. Without waiting for me to respond, she said, "My outside and insides are balanced! I feel inside just the way I act on the outside, and it feels so good!"

Like Katherine, many are becoming increasingly interested in using technology to support the brain. There are online guidelines for 'hacking the brain' by shooting electrical currents into it. There are devices that look like they come straight out of science fiction, but few have any research support, and I haven't seen any that match the evidence in support of Brainwave Optimization™.[21] It is the only technology I currently recommend as a tool to REPLACE! stress, worry, and anxiety with mindfulness. And the results are profound.

Need to Relax? Take Your Senses for a Walk

Did you know that you are a time traveler? It doesn't require science fiction or the suspension of disbelief at a movie theater in order to time travel. We travel through time constantly, by distorting time so that it seems to go much faster or much more slowly than usual. Unfortunately, in times of stress, it is the moments of worry and anxiety that seem to last forever, and it is difficult to ever get enough time to relax.

This next mindfulness strategy distorts time in your favor. It takes either four or four and half minutes, but it creates the positive illusion of a much longer time of relaxation. Though you can do this inside, it is most powerful when done outside, especially in nature, but it can increase relaxation when done in any environment. [22]

Sense Walk Exercise

Step outside and set the timer on your phone for one minute. During this minute you will put all your awareness on your visual field, using your internal voice to keep your focus on the details of what you are seeing. Asking yourself questions can help to direct your attention to more visual details. "Is the green of that leaf greener than the green of the grass?" How far into the horizon can I see? What are all of the colors I can see?" Or just let all the other senses recede into the background and for one minute focus all of your awareness on sight.

When your timer goes off, you will reset it for another minute which will be completely dedicated to hearing. You can close your eyes if you like, or just cock your head to the side and stare off into the distance. You can also walk if you like, as long as all of your awareness is focused on sounds.

When your timer goes off for the second time, you will again reset it for a minute. This next minute is dedicated to touch and feeling. Place your focus on your skin, hands, and feet. Touch and feel as much as you can in one minute, focusing on the feelings. Compare two "hard" objects for hardness or two softer objects for softness. Feel the air on your face. Touch and feel.

When your timer goes off for the third time, you have a choice. You can add the sense of taste in for 30 seconds if you wish. Be playful and taste the grass and the tree bark and anything else that you wish, just don't go licking strange mushrooms or fungi! You could be in for a totally different experience then. Or, instead of a taste-walk, move on to the final step.

The final minute is the crescendo. Focus on all the senses simultaneously. Push yourself to notice as much visual, auditory, and kinesthetic information as you can. It may feel overwhelming or overloading. 'Lean' into it, getting as much sensation as you can in one minute. See, hear, and touch.

Now that you have gone through the description of the exercise, find five minutes to go outside now and take a Sense Walk. You'll love it.

What did you think? Most people experience the time as seeming to be much longer than four or four and a half minutes. It is a wonderful way to relax in the middle of a day, especially a day spent inside in an office. It also trains your brain to be mindful of your senses all the time.

Mindfulness by Piggyback

This last strategy combines a mindfulness technique—scaling—with a strategy that is most accurately categorized into the EXERCISE! step because it is designed to help you remember to practice. It is a form of a Reminder Strategy, which you will learn about in the next section. I include it here because many of my clients have found the combined strategy to be very helpful in creating moments of calm and mindfulness in the middle of busy days.

The Piggyback Mindfulness strategy links moments of mindfulness to another habit that already occurs regularly during your day. This allows for easier integration of multiple moments of mindfulness, which then become their own habit. My clients have generally used one of two different habits for this strategy. One is a little more playful and edgy than the other; pick the one that feels right for you.

What do you already do multiple times every day? Two distinct possibilities present themselves. First, you almost certainly have a habit of eating multiple times a day, probably three times. Eating, then, is a perfect habit to piggyback your mindfulness on. One way to do so would be to pack your lunch into a brightly colored plastic bag with smiley faces on it. That way, every time you begin to eat, you remind yourself to check how calm and relaxed you feel. This is a Reminder Strategy, too, which links a moment of mindfulness into the neural network associated with your mealtimes.

If you see all those smiley faces on your lunch bag every time you begin to eat, you would remember that you wanted to check on your level of calm. To do so, you would use scaling questions, such as, "From one to ten, where one is not very calm (very stressed) and ten is very calm and relaxed, how calm do I feel right now?" Whatever your answer is, ask yourself how you could be one degree more relaxed? For example, if I feel like I am a "5" because I am halfway between stressed and relaxed, I would then ask myself, "How would I reach a 6 on the scale?" Often you will find that just asking the question will bring you closer to the next level of relaxation. (It is important to ask the question with the emphasis on "How calm?" rather than "How stressed?" to direct the mind's focus.)

The more playful and edgy approach would be to recognize that not only do you eat several times a day, you almost certainly go to the bathroom several times a day. You probably even go to the bathroom more often than you eat. This will especially be true if you are following the guidelines often given by health coaches and drinking lots of water. Instead of linking a moment of mindfulness to your mealtimes, you would link it to the moment you head to the bathroom or head back from it. Again, you would 'scale' your calm and relaxation and take one step to increase your level of relaxation. (If you are working from home and feeling playful and 'punny,' you could place a physical scale, one used for measuring weight, on your toilet seat. You would have to move it each time in order to use the toilet, and then you would 'scale' your relaxation, very probably with a smile on your face.)

Mindful Zombies

I find the idea of a mindful zombie to be quite amusing. It always brings a smile when I think of it. In this chapter, you have learned multiple approaches to catching your zombie-like habits and bringing moments of awareness to replace them. Ironically, you have also learned ways to make the mindfulness automatic, that is, more zombie-habit like. You are creating habits of mindfulness, a wonderful oxymoron.

Practice mindfulness as often as you can, and you will find surprising uses for it. I never thought I would use it to unintentionally scare a surgeon into almost stabbing me with his needle. On the other hand, how much more playful can you get?

CHAPTER TWENTY

METAPHORS:
ATLAS HOLDING UP THE WEIGHT OF THE
WORLD

Dealing with worry, stress, and anxiety wouldn't be so bad if you could shake them off whenever you wanted. True, it wouldn't be a walk in the park, but it could be more like an old knee injury that is more annoying than anything else. Unfortunately, bad moods are more like getting stuck in the mud and feeling like you're never going to get free. In this chapter, you will learn an important step in the REPLACE! process that will help free you whenever you "get stuck."

Often times, getting stuck in bad moods or pessimism is the result of the way we use metaphors to define whatever is happening in our lives. Because of this, it is imperative for you to learn how to fight off the invisible power of your unintentionally negative metaphors.

You can see the power of metaphors both negative and positive in a story about my friend Julia. She is a successful attorney in Washington, D.C. with a jet-setting lifestyle. In the years I have been friends with her on (and off) Facebook, I have seen her post from far-flung parts of the U.S. and the globe, including New Orleans, San Diego, Montana, Wyoming, British Columbia, Turkey, Western Sahara, England, Holland, Hawaii, and more. She is young, intelligent, attractive, and has close friends who share her taste for exotic adventures. She has a life many might envy.

She also has a life, and in particular a job, that anyone would agree has all the makings of stress and potential overwhelm. She works extremely long hours, often referencing "all nighters," nail-biting litigation, and cases where a mistake on her part would have drastic negative consequences for her clients.

Despite this, her Facebook posts are uniformly positive and upbeat, emphasizing her gratitude for her life and her friends while sharing positive aphorisms and inspiring pictures. Once, however, I saw a post from her that started out quite differently than most, and I asked her if I could share it. Here is how it read:

"As I was driving to work this morning with a few tears in my eyes, pretty substantial bags under my eyes, and feeling incredibly overwhelmed by the amount of tasks on my plate, I felt like Atlas with the weight of the world on my shoulders. . ."

This sentence powerfully captures feelings of stress and worry with a number of metaphors, most notably Atlas. Julia is not a Greek myth, of course, nor is she doomed to actually carry the world, but her metaphorical description revealed the pressure she felt throughout the day. Perhaps you have felt like she did, but used different language. Have you ever said to yourself or anybody else, "I feel like my world is coming to an end," "I feel like I'm just hanging on by a thread," "I feel like I'm walking a tightrope without a safety net," or any other of a dozen similar things?

Most achievers and people seeking success have said things like this at one time or another. If you have, then let me tell you what you were doing. You were doing two things. First, you were describing your internal experience as you best understood it at that moment. But you already knew that! That's what it felt like you were doing—simply expressing your feelings in a colorful way. But that's not all you were doing. You were also unknowingly "conspiring" with your brain to create and maintain a metaphor that kept you stuck in that experience and fed your habits of worry, stress, and anxiety.

In this chapter, you will learn a powerful REPLACE! step. You will learn how to replace metaphors you have associated with your old habits. Your new metaphors will propel you toward your goals instead of away from them. As you shift your disempowering metaphors, you will rewire your brain and support the new habits you are building.

The Power of Metaphors

It is easy to underestimate the power of metaphors because they are so commonplace. They are the framework we use in our language and the life's blood of every good speech or article. They are often sprinkled throughout conversations, making them even more difficult to see because they disappear into the background. Sometimes we use metaphors in a calculated manner, designing them intentionally to bulk up an argument or drive home a point, but equally often we blindly include them in our discussions without even having the awareness of them popping up.

This leads us to the $64,000 question—what is the upshot of all of this? Why should I even give a damn about metaphors?

It turns out that metaphors are an essential ingredient in our processing of the world. They are the invisible fabric used by our mental and linguistic systems, the scaffolding that we use to build new concepts or ideas. They provide a guide for navigating unfamiliar territory or situations. Any time we need a roadmap for a new experience, we depend on metaphors. Not only that, but they also assist us in decision making. They allow us to make snap judgments by filtering for the information that we think is important—that reflects our values—and leaving out the rest.

How many metaphors did you notice as you read the last three paragraphs? The content was an accurate description of the importance of metaphors, and it was expressed almost exclusively through metaphors. Go back and read the section again, this time with an eye for the metaphors. (That is a metaphor, too, of course.)

Notice how none of it was a literal description of the world. Metaphors are not physical, so they can't be a 'frame,' and they aren't 'blood.' Water is 'sprinkled,' not metaphors, and they are neither visible nor invisible so they can't 'disappear into a background.' Numbers are 'calculated,' not manners, and people 'bulk up,' not arguments. Nails are 'driven,' not points, and so on.

I intended there to be 24 unique metaphors in those three paragraphs; how many did you uncover?

Metaphors have a real impact on our lives, as they linger below our conscious awareness. One of the most common stress-causing metaphors is the language characterizing time in monetary terms. "Time is money" is the overarching concept, and it goes without notice when people talk of "spending time," "wasting time," or "running out of time." All of these depend on the metaphor, and make us automatically accept time as something that is limited and can be used as a resource.

This metaphor would not have been as natural before the Industrial Revolution, and it has significant implications for how we think about time. How much less stressed would you feel if you thought of time as a river that you were floating on? You are moving with the water, and it is always the present. In this metaphor, it doesn't even make sense to be "short on time" because you are always "going with the flow" of time. It may not be easy to shift your metaphor because of your habits, but it can still be helpful to realize that there are alternatives.

Taking Control of Your Metaphors

Your choice of metaphors is even more important when they are about you and your life. You may think of your metaphors as fixed in place— something you can't affect. But metaphors can be a form of visualization, and visualization is a tool you can control that has been shown to have a major impact on the brain. Here is an example of what can happen if you go with the metaphor, make it a vivid visualization, and then exercise control over it.

Jane is a client who came to me with concerns about stress and anxiety. Although she was also able to identify multiple resources and support systems, she couldn't seem to feel good about them. They seemed much less real to her than her problems. At the end of the first session, she said to me, "I feel like I am walking on a tightrope, and I don't even have one of those long pole thingies to help me balance." This was an expression of overwhelm, and the emotion was also visible in her face and body language.

I had her visualize that metaphor for a moment and notice how she felt. I could see her facial muscles tighten while she shifted nervously from side to side. She said that her stress in that moment was a seven on a one-to-ten scale.

I then had her imagine that there were two more tightropes on either side of her at shoulder height. By reaching upwards, she could grip these lines to support herself while she walked the tightrope. In this new version of the metaphor, she was still balancing on a tightrope but she had extra support. I knew that this reflected her larger beliefs about the world overall. She did believe that she was in a challenging situation, but she also believed that she had many resources available to her.

I could see the immediate power of the strategy by looking at her. She smiled and sat up straighter. Just by taking control of her metaphor, she immediately felt much better. The situation didn't need to change for her emotions to change. She was able to create a metaphor that reminded her of her true assessment of her overall situation. That changed her emotional state and reduced her stress immediately, while reducing the negative impact on her brain. In turn, this increased her immediate willingness to access her available resources—to "lean" on them. Exerting control over this metaphor allowed her to make better decisions and break out of a state of inaction. Within minutes she stated that her stress was at a level two, and she identified concrete plans she could use to improve her situation.

There are three steps to the process of metaphor control. Each is important.

1. Visualize the metaphor and notice how you feel.

2. Take control of the metaphor and change it to reflect what you really believe about the overall situation.

3. Notice how you feel while visualizing the new metaphor.

The more vividly you engage with the new metaphor, the more power it will have. Engage it in your communication with yourself and others, and you will multiply its power. Begin to think in terms of the new metaphor.

Just as the brain is influenced by present-tense language, it is also highly influenced by your metaphors—especially what you claim to be true about yourself. You can think of these as metaphors about your identity, or who you really are. Your brain will find information in your experience to support whatever metaphor you claim as your own. It will find evidence that you are "at the end of your rope," "hanging by a thread," or that you "have the world on a string." Similar types of metaphors create very different emotions.

As you practice your FIND! and INTERRUPT! steps, remember to apply them to your metaphors. You can then engage this latest strategy to REPLACE! any disempowering metaphors with new, powerful ones.

Here is a final example. I was talking to an entrepreneur. he said that she felt like she was on a log in a log-balancing contest, and the log was spinning out of control underneath her. That expressed how she was feeling in her life and her business at that time. I said to her, "Go with that!" I had her visualize it and notice how she felt when she visualized it.

Then I told her to control her metaphor. She changed the image so that she was still in a log-balancing contest, but it was only in two inches of water on a bouncy floating raft! And she was wearing her bathing suit! If she fell off, no problem! She was learning in a safe environment. She was committed to "getting" this log. I knew that reflected what she really believed about her business much more accurately than the first metaphor. The fit with her larger beliefs allowed her to accept the new metaphor even though it wasn't how she had previously felt. Then, by imagining the new metaphor, she changed how she was feeling, and it brought her back into alignment with her vision for herself and her business.

Summary

Metaphors rule your life. You can't communicate with others or with yourself without metaphors. You can't talk or write without resorting to metaphors. The metaphors you choose create invisible boundaries and filters for your experience of the world. If you don't challenge and intentionally choose and control your metaphors, you will find it more difficult to wipe out worry, stress, and anxiety. To achieve your goals, you must increase your awareness of your metaphors and of your power over them.

Whenever you find yourself describing your situation in a metaphor that may express how you feel in the moment but doesn't serve you in the long term, remember to follow these simple steps:
1. Take control of the metaphor and change it to reflect what you really believe about the overall situation.
2. Notice how you feel while visualizing the new metaphor.
3. You'll find that you feel a lot better.

That was certainly true for my friend Julia, who understands how her brain works. Here is the entirety of her Facebook post, a fabulous example for all of us:

"As I was driving to work this morning with a few tears in my eyes, pretty substantial bags under my eyes, and feeling incredibly overwhelmed by the amount of tasks on my plate, I felt like Atlas with the weight of the world on my shoulders.

As I pulled into the parking garage, I just decided I have to make this light and easy. And so I envisioned Atlas lightly tossing and catching the world on his shoulders as easily as if it were a beach ball. Nice and easy, light and playful, and with a smile on his face. I instantly felt lifted.

Throughout the day, as I've found myself stressed (and not breathing), I just returned to that vision of Atlas gently tossing the ball and catching it. . . tossing it and catching it. . . moving lightly and easily through the next task.

I still have a lot to do, but it's a lot more pleasant to do it without the weight of the world on my shoulders."

SECTION FIVE

EXERCISE!

CHAPTER TWENTY-ONE

INTRODUCTION TO THE EXERCISE! STEP

Beauty fades. Roses droop. Leaves fall. And good intentions and willpower are not sustained unless habits are created. That is why the final step in the FIRE! process, the "E" for EXERCISE!, is so important.

You can think of this step by other names, such as "Habituate" or "Condition" or "Turn Into a Habit." You may already realize that this is not really a new step. You have already started on this step every time you have done an exercise in this book, every time you practice a new strategy, and every time you remember to do something new instead of the actions of your old habits of worry, stress, and anxiety. Every new step is an instance in the process of EXERCISE!. Every step builds toward a new habit.

This process is based on the basic brain principles outlined in the book so far. Every time a neural network fires off, it also wires at least a little bit. Every single time you've done a full repetition of the first three steps of FIND!, INTERRUPT!, and REPLACE!, you have been wiring in a new neural network and locking in your habits. Even if you have only completed one of these steps in any given moment of worry, stress, or anxiety, this effort has contributed to your new habits. Every opportunity matters! In situations where you have previously engaged in worry, stress, or anxiety, there are only two options; you either further wire in the old habit or you do not.

Each step of the FIRE! process makes its own contribution to change. When you have used the strategies of the FIND! step, you have changed the previous neural network. By celebrating, and by changing your focus to include the sensory channels, you have wired new neurons into the previous neural network. This has changed it, at least a little, every time. Just that process by itself makes it a little easier to get out from under the power of the old habits.

Similarly, every time that you have used strategies from the INTERRUPT! step to interrupt the old habits, you have kept the neurons from wiring together and led them to wire apart. This has also weakened the old habit. Lastly, every successful strategy from the REPLACE! step has strengthened a new network and lessened the old one.

The success of the first three steps can also work against you, though. The very momentum that you create by using the FIND!, INTERRUPT!, and REPLACE! can make things seem sustainable even before they really are. That is why the EXERCISE! step is so important. You have begun to alter the habits, but you have not yet wiped them out completely. To move beyond the frustration of worry, stress, and anxiety, you need to train yourself. Thinking about this like an exercise and diet regime, you could say that you have lost the weight of these habits, so to speak, but now you must keep it off.

The chapters in the EXERCISE! section will help you "keep the weight off." They offer a variety of approaches to assist you in conditioning in the new, useful habits. In these short chapters, you will encounter frameworks, inspiring examples, and strategies to make it as easy as possible for you to complete the journey you started the first time you took off your shoe and committed to change. You're almost home!

CHAPTER TWENTY-TWO

STAGES OF LEARNING

How does a "dance floor dunce" turn into a "dancing fool?" Through practical brain science, of course! My experience with this transformation serves as a fun (although sometimes personally painful) illustration of the process of habit change. I use it here to give you another way to understand your own transformation before you move into the final step of the FIRE! process.

To prepare you for the EXERCISE! step, it will be helpful for you to have a greater understanding of the steps to lasting, personal change. The "Stages of Learning" framework will help you understand the way you develop from an old habit to a new one. This framework applies to development in any area of life, and it will be particularly helpful as you continue to lock in the empowering behaviors outlined in this book.[23] It can help you know when you need to focus more on one of the first three steps and when you are ready to put your focus primarily on this last step: EXERCISE!.

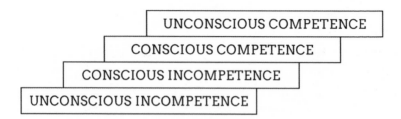

As you can see in the illustration, the "Stages of Learning" framework is a four-stage process. The first stage is the stage of Unconscious Incompetence. In regards to outgrowing worry, stress, and anxiety, you were probably in this first stage when you discovered this book. This is the stage where you were incompetent, but you didn't know the cause of your own mistakes or poor performance. You may even have been so unconscious about your unhelpful worry and stress that you didn't realize that you had any control over it at all.

My experience in learning to dance demonstrates the framework well. I loved to dance, but no one loved to dance with me! I was terrible! My enthusiasm was my only savior, as long as I pretended not to notice the pitying looks. I had always been told I had no rhythm and no talent at dancing. I didn't even know when I was off the beat, because I couldn't hear it in the music. I was in the first stage of learning—Unconscious Incompetence. I was bad, and I often didn't even know it until someone pointed it out to me. That was part of the problem. Does this sound familiar to you?

Even though it felt impossible to learn to dance, I knew enough about the brain to resist the temptation to write myself off. I threw myself into the challenge, sometimes dancing every night in the week. This accelerated my progress, as well as resulting in sore feet and a greater list of those who threatened to wear protective footwear whenever I was on the dance floor.

The next stage is Conscious Incompetence. At this stage in my dance education, I was still bad, but I knew it. I wouldn't always admit it, but at least I knew. Even more importantly, I was beginning to be conscious of what I was doing. I didn't always need the sidelong glances of others to tell me when I as off beat. I could tell. I could tell when I wasn't following the steps of a dance by something other than the feeling of my partner's toe under my heel. I was aware not only of my incompetence but somewhat aware of what I needed to do instead, even if I couldn't yet pull it off. In my mind, I could see myself becoming an actual dancer.

The FIND! process is designed to bridge these first two stages, to bring you from Unconscious Incompetence to Conscious Incompetence. Your commitment to the Celebrate Awareness strategy wires your brain to become aware of early signs of anxiety and of unproductive worry and stress. You may not always be able to shift in the moment, but you probably notice what you are doing. You accept that you have a role in creating the emotions, and you have increased insight into your habitual sensory channels and how they create the worry, stress, and anxiety. You are aware of the negative cycle of beating yourself up for your feelings, and you break that cycle by celebrating instead.

The next stage is Conscious Competence. As a dancer, this is the stage where I was able to dance and stay on the beat, but only when I stayed very focused. I would have to remind myself of the next move, pay attention to the steps, and sometimes even count them in my head. The count of the Lindy Hop—"one, two, three and four, five, six, seven and eight" rang in my head as I spun and turned on the dance floor. This stage was more enjoyable for my dance partners, and for me, but it still felt like hard work. If I let my attention waver for a moment, to just enjoy the music, I would fall back into old bad habits, miss a step, get off beat, or be in danger of kicking my partner.

The INTERRUPT! and REPLACE! steps help you move to Conscious Competence. You may still have to focus and remember to interrupt yourself when you notice signs of worry, stress, or anxiety, but you are able to replace them and be more productive. You are able to stay calm in stressful situations, although it may take effort to do so. You may find that you have little energy left after a day of stress, even if you managed to eliminate any anxiety and only use worry and stress appropriately. Just the effort of focus and consciously interrupting and replacing your old habits will require energy, although it is energy you will be grateful you spent.

The Unconscious Dancer

If you have followed the recommendations in this book and completed the exercises at every point, then you will likely be in the Conscious Competence stage right now. You will have used the FIND! step to be conscious and the INTERRUPT! and REPLACE! steps to be competent. You are now a consciously competent "dancer" in stressful situations, even ones that place heavy demand on your resources. This is a much more enjoyable experience than being unconsciously incompetent, worried, stressed, and anxious. Many people stop at this stage, believing that they have accomplished their goals.

However, there is a fourth stage—one that is even more enjoyable. This is the stage of Unconscious Competence. Even with all of my focus on the importance of awareness, you may have noticed the many references to "building new habits" in order to replace old ones. You don't want to always have to depend on awareness. As you achieve sufficient repetition with your replacements, and with high emotional intensity, you will find that your brain moves to the replacement automatically instead of to the old response. If you get enough emotional intensity, especially strong playfulness, this may happen with relatively little repetition. You may not even notice the absence of the old worry or stress response until someone points it out to you. That would be an indication that you were unconscious, unaware—in a zombie-like habit state. That used to be a bad thing, but now it is a good thing! You have harnessed the positive power of habit.

As I continued to dance regularly, I began to notice times when my focus could shift away from the steps and move to my partner and the music. Previously, this would have caused me to lose the beat. But at that point in my development, I was able to stay with the rhythm unconsciously and allow my conscious awareness to do something else. This is the goal of repetition with emotional intensity: to get to this point, this state of unconsciously performing your new, desired habits. The EXERCISE! step will get you there!

CHAPTER TWENTY-THREE

CAN THE EFFECTS OF CELEBRATION LAST?

It may not always be easy to accept that such a simple and playful practice as celebration can have a lasting impact. It is one of the questions many of my clients have had as they entered the EXERCISE! step, wondering if their brains would continue to benefit from constant celebration. I certainly understand if you have had this question as well, and simply urge you to do a quick touchdown dance after you read these next two stories.

"Way To Go, Brain!"

I clearly remember a day just before I created the Celebrate Awareness strategy. As I rolled to a halt at the first stop sign on my street, I slapped my forehead. "Not again," I thought, "I'm an idiot," realizing that I had left behind the lunch I had packed for work. The night before, I had carefully laid out time to prepare a meal I really love. It was going to be a treat to myself in the middle of another full day.

But I did what was so common for me at that point: I left it on my counter, just as I had left a vital document the day before, and my office key the day before that.

Back then my forehead was getting sore from my palm, and my nerves were getting worn thin from my constant forgetting and the self-berating that would rush over me once I realized my mistakes. I had zero patience for myself. As you now know, I was making my memory worse without even knowing it. I was "teaching my dog not to come home."

So much has changed for me since I started practicing Celebrate Awareness regularly. Sure, I remember things better, but that hasn't been the most significant result. What really amazes me is my new habits of response on the occasions when I do forget something.

I left my lunch on the counter recently, just as I had in the past. I was just approaching that first stop sign when I remembered. But now my automatic response was playfulness and gratitude that I had remembered when I did. I found myself saying, "I have a great brain!" and "Way to go, brain!" I was very aware of how much better it was that I remembered it at that point, instead of forgetting it altogether. I even did a little jig as I ran into the house to get my lunch.

Cumulatively, these changed moments have had a huge positive effect on me. Instead of regularly having small moments of frustration, I now have an equal number of small moments of celebration. They add up to a significant increase in happiness. And they happen, so it feels, without any effort at all. I no longer need to be conscious of the FIND! step; the behavior has changed to take care of itself.

When You Live With A Bad Smell Long Enough, You Can't Tell It's There

According to Charles Duhigg's wonderful book, *The Power of Habit*, when you live with a bad smell long enough, you can't tell it's there.[24] The world-renowned product Febreze almost failed because of this fact. They had a great product, they had a market, and the market had what seemed like a very clear need. But it turned out that everyone who needed deodorizing spray—someone living in a house with the cloying odor created by the urine of nine indoor cats, or a park ranger whose main duty was trapping and releasing skunks—didn't find the smells they were immersed in to be offensive. In fact, these people hardly noticed them.

What is this inability to be aware of one's own plight but a parallel form of Unconscious Incompetence? In other words, these folks were in bad shape, they didn't notice that fact, and they therefore were in desperate need of the FIND! step.

How did the manufacturers solve this problem? Their researchers discovered something very interesting as they studied the difference between people who had a consistent habit of cleaning their house and the people who cleaned occasionally, in massive cleaning sprees, but who didn't have a consistent habit. The difference was that those with the consistent habit had a regular moment of celebration, of satisfaction, at the end of each part of their cleaning routine. This moment of feeling good became the reward for cleaning. These regular cleaners craved that feeling, and therefore they kept on cleaning. In this way, cleaning became a habit. When the Febreze marketing team connected their product to that rewarding moment at the end of cleaning, it immediately took off.

How does this apply to the EXERCISE! step? You can easily expand celebration throughout your day so that you condition your replacement behaviors until they become habits. You are already accustomed to celebrating your awareness of the indicators of worry, stress, and anxiety in the FIND! step. You can now extend your celebration practice in order to reward yourself for every success. Every time you implement an INTERRUPT! or REPLACE! strategy, you can celebrate. It will turn this final step of the FIRE! process into the easiest EXERCISE! you have ever done. The celebration will last and last!

CHAPTER TWENTY-FOUR

REMEMBERING TO EXERCISE!

Fortunately you don't have to go to the gym to do the EXERCISE! step, but there are some simple strategies to help you implement it on a daily basis. As an extra bonus, you will see that you can easily apply these strategies, what I call "Reminder Strategies," to help you get your body into shape too!

Whenever I think of these strategies I think of the old proverb of how a kingdom was lost because of the lack of a horseshoe nail for a horse:

For want of a nail the shoe was lost.
For want of a shoe the horse was lost.
For want of a horse the rider was lost.
For want of a rider the message was lost.
For want of a message the battle was lost.
For want of a battle the kingdom was lost.
And all for the want of a horseshoe nail.

The Reminder Strategies are the 'horseshoe nails' that hold together the steps of the FIRE! process. In your case, they help you win, not lose, your 'kingdom' of a life without unproductive worry, stress, and anxiety. I think you'll really love them!

Reminder Strategies

You can easily predict when you would use Reminder Strategies just based on the name. You use these strategies when you haven't yet interrupted the old habits sufficiently to allow you to remember to use your new strategies. This may be the case for a while. You may find yourself doing the old habits of worry, stress, and anxiety before you remember to implement the FIND! and INTERRUPT! steps.

Here is a stress example that will resonate with most people. Suppose that you have had a bad habit of getting 'stressed out' while driving. I will suppose that it is such a habit, an automatic behavior, that you don't even notice the increasing stress until you begin to yell at other drivers, honk the horn, or aggressively handle the car. You are embarrassed and are committed to changing this behavior, but you haven't yet figured out how to remember to stay calm and use your strategies. What would you do? Take a moment and think about it for yourself. You can use strategies you have learned in this book or elsewhere.

A very common, but often ineffective, strategy is to use a written reminder. Some people might post a small note on their dashboard that says, "Take a deep breath and be mindful! Remember why it is so important for you stay calm while you drive! You want to be a good example for your children and come home safely to them!" Obviously you must have kids for this note to have any impact, but you get the idea. That said, a message like this is hardly effective enough to make a lasting impact on road rage or the intense stresses of driving through rush hour traffic, breathing in lung-fulls of exhaust, and trying not to get cut off or run down by a semi. With what you now know about neuroscience, you can take this simple reminder strategy much further, thereby making it much more impactful.

So how do you do that? As you probably realize now, your brain is very good at not continuing to pay attention to messages in the environment. There is too much input for your brain to focus on everything around you, and it therefore must prioritize information it's taking in. If you were to just put a sign like this in your car and then go on your way, the sign might not have enough emotional intensity to get prioritized. If that were the case, it would likely only work when it was new and you kept it in your conscious awareness.

Fortunately, there are three Reminder Strategies that you could use to remember to be mindful and break the old habit of stressed-out driving. The first would be to make the sign very unusual. Your brain is used to seeing unimportant written messages and therefore may not be quick to pay attention to them. But if you make the message unusual, you can change that. There are many ways to do this, keeping in mind the principle that the brain is most likely to process new and unusual information. You could make the sign brightly colored. You could change the sign each day. You could use the "shoe principle" and write the information on something that would not ordinarily be in your car, like a whiteboard, or on something that might be in your car but wouldn't ordinarily have a message on it, like a brown paper bag. You are using the principle of catching your brain's attention. You want your brain to be highlighting that input over other information it's processing. As in the case of your shoe, you want your brain to be asking, "What is that message doing there?" In fact, the shoe itself is a Reminder Strategy.

The second Reminder Strategy is to take steps to give the message a high level of emotional intensity. If you associate celebration to the reminder from the very beginning, you will be much more likely to continue to notice it. Someone who did not have your understanding of the brain might just hang such a note on her steering wheel or put it on the dashboard of her car, and expect for it to be effective. But you now know better!

If you were to do this, you might instead take such a sign, put on your headphones with some of your favorite high-energy music, and dance your way to your car shaking the sign triumphantly in the air all the way. When you hang the sign in your car you might drink a champagne toast to it, proclaiming loudly to it that it is the best sign ever! You might do an exaggerated "salaam" to it, bowing down and shouting "You da sign! No! You are da sign!" You understand that the purpose of all of such "silliness" is to ramp up the emotional intensity of the neural network connected to that sign. The more playful, the more effective the reminder. As with the example of skipping in an earlier section, just reading this paragraph likely brought a smile to your face. You can easily imagine how much more likely you will be to notice the sign when you get in the car having made such a strong connection to it. You would reinforce this connection by celebrating your awareness every time you did notice the sign and then follow through by creating the calmness and mindfulness that will assist you on your drive.

The third approach to a powerful reminder is not to use a written message at all. As we discussed earlier, symbols and metaphors can be even more powerful than words. An example from one of my clients provides a funny and powerful illustration. She realized that much of her stress came from habits of mindless activities that distracted her from her productivity. She realized that she watched television much more than she had previously noticed and that she was on autopilot while doing so. She often wasn't even conscious of having sat down to watch until she was already doing it. Then she had to overcome the inertia and the temptation to just keep doing what she was doing.

She found a simple solution by putting a blanket over the television. This meant that she couldn't run through the movements of her old habit as she had. She couldn't just sink into the couch and click on the remote. She actually found herself regularly doing just that, only to notice that she couldn't see because of the blanket covering the screen! That gave her a moment of conscious awareness, and she was able to immediately celebrate, starting the FIND! step, and then continue the steps from there. You can also think of this Reminder Strategy as designed to make it more difficult to be unconsciously incompetent. It forces consciousness, and then you have the choice to be consciously competent. In the example we have been using, you could do something that would prevent you from driving, such as covering the steering wheel. That would be your reminder to take a moment of mindfulness and reflection on the values you wished to follow while you drove.

You now have three different approaches to implementing the Reminder strategy to allow you to get the most out of your naturally-occurring opportunities to practice your replacement behaviors. By putting up these reminders, and using emotional intensity so your brain will continue to notice them, you will enable yourself to remember to regularly follow the FIND!, INTERRUPT!, and REPLACE! steps in your daily life.

CHAPTER TWENTY-FIVE

GET MORE EXERCISE! WITH PRACTICE

If you want to accelerate your development of any new habit, you need to have lots of opportunities for repetition. Sometimes, however, enough opportunities to practice your strategies just don't arise in your daily life. That is why it is equally important to use the EXERCISE! step in created situations, like role-play and mental rehearsal. By this, I simply mean practice.

When you follow the recommendations in this book, you exercise your new habits like a basketball player would practice a new shooting approach or a golfer a new swing. They are not playing for results during practice, but each repetition helps them immensely during game day. With you, it will be the same. As you practice your strategies in fabricated situations, you can become more and more accustomed to performing your new strategies, behaviors, and habits. You may even have thought about these previous exercises in exactly that way, as "practice." Whenever you have done the assignments from a chapter, you have consciously decided to develop a new behavior through practice

A great place to do this is in your car. I mentioned in an earlier story that I created the Thought Cavalry process because I found myself with a habit of worry and negative emotions when I was driving. Even if you don't have that habit, you can still use your time in the car to apply the EXERCISE! step with great power.

Remembering To Practice In Your Car

The car is a great location for practice because it is a setting where your brain is already a little on autopilot. You probably already let your mind drift or think about a variety of topics during a routine drive. Commutes by bus or train give you even more leeway to focus your mind on helpful practice.

Here is a playful example that integrates elements from several strategies that are familiar to you. As you read this strategy, vividly imagine what I describe. This will prepare you for practicing the Thought Cavalry, Fades, and Scrambles in your car. (This exercise will need to be modified if you don't have a car. With every example I give of a car, replace it with your commute by subway, bus, train, bike, etc. If you don't commute to work, perhaps you could imagine your morning shower.)

Imagine your car. Picture the exact location where it is parked. Imagine the likely details of the next time you will get in your car. Identify the time of day and the likely weather. Make up the details if you are unsure.

Imagine that you are walking toward your car. Just before you reach it, hear the sound of the cavalry bugle in your mind. Look around for the source of the bugle sound. Where is it? You can't find the source of it anywhere. As you take the final step toward your car, you hear the cavalry sound again! Imagine looking around again and only seeing what you would normally see—your street, driveway, or garage.

Unlock your car, open the door, and jump backwards in surprise! There is a cavalry troop in your car! They start as tiny figures and expand as they fly out of the door. Imagine horses all around you rearing up and neighing happily and enthusiastically. The bugle sound is going on and on. The riders are circling the car and cheering for you. Even the horses seem to be cheering. You jump into the car. As the the car door closes, you can see the cavalry shrink down and fly through the opening, shrinking into microscopic size as they enter the car. Imagine hearing a tiny sound of cheering accompanied by the bugle call.

If you vividly followed along with the guided imagery, then it will very likely affect you the next time you get into your car. Some element in your environment will trigger the memory of this visualization. You will then you have the opportunity to implement any of your strategies. If you wanted to practice a Thought Cavalry strategy, then you would intentionally search for an unproductive worry or stressful thought and use it to begin the strategy.

Interrupt the thought, replace it, and go on your way.

To practice a Visual Fade, you would bring up a painful memory. Then follow the Fade guidelines to pull it up and push it away, fading it over and over until the emotion is sufficiently diminished.

To practice a Scramble, just ask yourself, "What have I said to myself in worry or stress situations?" As you soon as hear one of these internal comments or voices, follow it with your favorite scramble. Or use one of mine. It becomes automatic as you practice it. You are creating a new neural network that will become its own habit.

Bring In Friends To Help You EXERCISE!

You can also enlist your friends, family, and colleagues to assist in role-play exercises that will practice the new replacements. When I left one of my companies and I was out on my own, I was put in a situation to do more sales and enrollment conversations than I ever had before. I realized I was creating stress, and even anxiety, as I anticipated those conversations. By implementing the sensory channel questions from the FIND! step, I discovered that my primary negative sensory channel was imagining critical responses from my potential clients. I then set out to change the neural networks connected with those responses.

I asked several friends to join me in a 30-minute phone call. I told them about the kind of responses that I imagined and asked them to also create lists of critical, negative, or rejecting comments that could possibly be made by clients. I asked them to be realistic and also less realistic, more outrageous. During the 30-minute phone call, we did a rapid-fire role-play. They peppered me with critical and rejecting comments while I used my Power Poses and Power Moves to activate the neural networks of confidence and optimism. By the end of the 30 minutes, I had achieved my goal. Whenever I thought about or heard a critical comment, I was also reminded of my confidence and optimism. I had rewired my brain to connect the rejecting comments with feelings of empowerment. These feelings would then lead me to take more action toward my goals. I had managed to transform the emotional pain of rejection into its opposite—a feeling of playfulness and power that fueled my success.

Final Tips for Successful EXERCISE!

One final tip: practice in many different contexts and locations. As you practice with high emotional intensity, elements of the context and location will become connected to the neural network created by the practice. This increases the likelihood that you will remember to activate the strategy in that context or location when you really need it.

One final, final tip. Really! There's an old joke about the tourist lost in New York who stops a local and asks, "How do I get to Carnegie Hall?" The answer? "Practice, practice, practice!" Whether or not you've ever heard of the famous New York performance hall, you can take the advice to heart. Go out and practice, . . . (you know the rest!).

SECTION SIX

NEXT STEPS

CHAPTER TWENTY-SIX

YOUR NEW BEST FRIEND, YOUR BRAIN

We began with the end in mind, so it is only fitting for us to end with the beginning in mind. You remember taking your shoe off to symbolize your commitment to change? This time let's do it just a little bit differently.

Take your brain out right now, and put it on your desk. If there is no desk in front of you, then put your brain on the nearest bookcase, or just hold it out in front of you with one hand as you hold this book with the other. (I can't know whether you ever physically put your shoe on your desk, but I know for sure that you imagined it. In any case, you have permission to use only your imagination this time— no brain surgery tools required.)

Pick up your brain in your hand. Feel the heft of it. Maybe notice the traces from where it sat on the desk. See it as you never have before. This brain can be the entry into a new world any time you wish.

You can build that world with your new knowledge, and you are the only one who can do it.

Imagine for a moment that you could compare this brain in your hand to the one you started this book with. What might you notice? Perhaps you would notice that the posterior cingulate has grown and your amygdala has shrunk from your meditation and mindfulness practice. Perhaps your basal ganglia has developed due to the new habits you have formed. Perhaps you have recovered from some prior shrinkage in the medial prefrontal cortex as your stress has reduced.

You may have no idea of where to look as I mention these brain areas. That's fine; this book has never been about the details of brain anatomy. It has always been about playfulness and practical results. And the practical results from your reading of this book and doing the exercises can't be seen (even with the imagination) by looking at the outside of your brain.

The most important changes would only appear visually in the connectivity between neurons, in your neural networks. Neurons that used to fire together, as you were worried, stressed, and anxious, have no longer been doing so. They have been firing apart and therefore wiring apart. New patterns of neurons have been firing together and thus wiring together. These neural networks are the new habits you've created in each of the four steps of the FIRE! process. They are the most important features of your new brain.

Go ahead and put your brain back inside your skull. You have a brand new relationship with your brain. Over the course of this book, you have worked with it, talked to it, complimented it, encouraged it, and now imagined holding it in your hand. It's good that you are better friends now. Because a brain, especially a stress-free brain, is a good friend to have.

Friends are Even Better in a Community

Where will you and your brain go from here? You may wish to review specific strategies in this book. The EXERCISE! step is continual; you can always benefit from continuing to practice. I encourage you to revisit the strategies in a variety of ways. You can go back to your favorite strategies—the ones that gave you the most joy and the best results. That's always fun. You can also go back to the strategies that didn't feel comfortable for you the first time through. You may find that they are easier or more fitting for you now.

You may also find that the best way to get the most from a second trip through the book is to do it with someone else. Teaching strategies is the best way to learn them. I know that from personal experience! You may find that you also hold yourself to a higher standard when you are teaching someone else. That, too, I know from personal experience.

You may also be interested in following the principles of this book in a virtual community setting through one of my programs. The principles are currently taught in my virtual program, *30 Days to Worry-Free Achievement*. You can find out more about that at my website, www.braincoachbrad.com. It can be very powerful to space the strategies out over a 30-

day period and both receive and provide support from others as you all work through the program together.

Whatever you do, and however you do it, I hope you will let me know about your results. You can leave your comments and experiences on my website or in reviews of the book online. You can inspire others with your results. Perhaps they will take their shoe off and start their journey because you did it first.

Now go out there and FIRE! your neurons! Use your brain for good. I'm proud of you.

[1] (P. 25) Ansell, Emily B. et al. 2012. "Cumulative Adversity and Smaller Gray Matter Volume in Medial Prefrontal, Anterior Cingulate, an Insula Regions," *Biological Psychiatry*. 72: 1, 57-64.

[2] (p. 26) American Psychological Association, "Stress Effects on the Body," www.apa.org. Accessed: 09/21/15.

[3] (P. 27) Holt-Lunstad J, et al. 2010 "Social Relationships and Mortality Risk: A Meta-analytic Review," *PLoS Med* 7: 7: e1000316. doi:10.1371/journal.pmed.1000316

[4] (P. 27) Clay, R.A. 2011. "Stressed in America," *Monitor on Psychology*. 42: 1, 60.

[5] (P. 30) www.unworriedbrain.com & www.braincoachbrad.com

[6] (P. 30) You will notice that in the previous sentence I used an odd manner of speaking, that is, talking about your brain as if it is distinct from you. I will talk about "working with your brain," "teaching your brain," "rewarding your brain," and so on.

Naturally, this brings up many philosophical questions, not the least of which are those of personal identity and the difference between the brain, the mind, and the self. Although I have spent many days and evenings discussing such fascinating questions with friends, colleagues, and in particular with my wife, Norah, who is a professor of philosophy, those questions are outside the main focus of this book. This book is focused on strategy and application, with just enough inclusion of science and frameworks for you to be able to successfully implement the recommendations. I strive to always "keep the end in mind" and focus on the goal: that you will learn to wipe out unproductive and unhelpful worry, stress, and anxiety in your life.

For that purpose, it is sometimes useful to speak about your brain as if it is not you. I will sometimes go so far as to speak about your brain as distinct not only from your conscious awareness, but as a committee working together on your behalf. This is a playful figure of speech, but one that can be helpful in providing an explanation for your internal experience. It also may not be as far-fetched as one might think, taking into consideration some of the split-brain research of Michael Gazzaniga. But again, those questions are outside of the scope of this book. See Gazzaniga, Michael *Tales From Both Sides of the Brain* (New York: Ecco, 2015). Remember the importance of playfulness and always keep your end goals in mind as you read the book, and as you use the recommended strategies to improve your life.

[7] (p. 31) The brain has multiple maps of the body, for sensory input and for movement. For a great discussion of this, see Blakeslee, Sandra and Blakeslee, Matthew, *The Body Has a Mind of its Own* (New York: Random House, 2008).

[8] (P. 32) See Doidge, Norman *The Brain That Changes Itself* (New York: Penguin Books, 2007) and Doidge, Norman *The Brain's Way of Healing* (New York: Viking, 2015).

[9] (P. 32) I will acknowledge that the simplicity of this phrase conceals depths, and it could be explained with sophisticated terminology and details of brain functioning. I will stay closer to its surface meaning and ask for forgiveness from you the reader if you wish a more detailed level of description, which is available in many other books about neuroscience. I particularly recommend Doidge, *The Brain That Changes Itself*.

[10] (P. 32) This very simple discussion omits the chemical messengers, neurotransmitters, that allow for impulses to pass between neurons. I am keeping it simple for the majority of readers.

[11] (P. 34) See the wonderful discussion of 'EP' in Duhigg, Charles *The Power of Habit* (New York: Random House, 2012).

[12] (P. 35) Smith, Kyle S. et al. 2012. "Reversible online control of habitual behavior by ontogenetic perturbation of medial prefrontal cortex," PNAS. 109: 46, 18932-18937.

[13] (P. 36) The term 'anxiety,' as it is popularly used, covers a variety of different emotional experiences. Some 'anxiety' is better thought of as excitement, but most uses of the term refer either to out of control worry or to inappropriate activation of the fear response. In any case, while I will discuss productive and useful worry and stress, I will not do the same for anxiety, because anxiety is never useful.

[14] (P. 115) Ophir, Eyal. Et al. 2009. "Cognitive Control in Media Multitaskers," PNAS. 106: 37, 15583-15587.

[15] (P.124) Boulenger, Veronique. Et al. 2010. "Interwoven functionality of the brain's action and language systems," The Mental Lexicon. 5: 2, 231-254.

[16] (P. 130) Kross, Ethan. Et al. 2014. "Self-Talk as a Regulatory Mechanism: How You Do It Matters," Journal of Personality and Social Psychology. 106: 2, 304-324.

[17] (P.136) Here's a fun read about something of extreme powers of meditators - Cromie, William J., 2002. "Meditation Changes Temperatures: Mind Controls Body in Extreme Experiments," Harvard University Gazette. April 18, 2002.

[18] (P. 136) Holzel, Britta K. Et al. 2011. "Mindfulness practice leads to increases in regional brain gray matter density," Psychiatry Research: Neuroimaging. 191: 1, 36-43.

[19] (P. 137) Bays, Jan Chozen, How to Train a Wild Elephant: And Other Adventures in Mindfulness (Boston: Shambala Publications, Inc., 2011).

[20] (P.138) Davidson, Richard J., and Begley, Sharon, The Emotional Life of Your Brain (New York: Hudson Street Press, 2012).

[21] (P.146) The research into Brainwave Optimization, which is known technically as "HIRREM," for High

Resolution, Relational, Resonance-based, Electroencephalic Mirroring, is well summarized at the website of Wake Forest Baptist Medical Center where Dr. Charles Tegeler and his team have been studying it extensively. http://www.wakehealth.edu/Research/Neurology/HIRREM/Research/Research.htm. Accessed: 09/21/15.

[22] (P.147) The Sense Walk exercise emphasizes the senses of sight, hearing, and touch (and is written as if assumes the ability to walk) but it can be done with limitations to any of the senses. Either replace the missing sense with taste or skip it altogether, adding more time to the other senses.

[23] (P. 166) This framework is used extensively in the fields of leadership and personal development, and rarely cited. For an interesting 'deep dive' into the framework, and for information on the controversy of its origins, I recommend reading the history of the tool at this website: http://www.businessballs.com/consciouscompetencelearningmodel.htm#conscious-competence-theory-origins. Accessed: 09/21/15.

[24] (P. 174) Charles Duhigg, *The Power of Habit* (New York: Random House, 2012). This is my favorite book on the science of habit formation.

ACKNOWLEDGEMENTS

I was eight years old when I promised my father I would write a book. He doesn't remember this, but I still do. In the ensuing years there have many people who encouraged me in my writing or my clinical and coaching work. There is no way I can list them all here. Fortunately, I have a solution. If you are reading this with the knowledge that you should be on the list, but you can't find your name, I have a request for you. Please use the power of your brain one more time, to visualize that you see your name printed here, exactly where it should be. Then celebrate!

The list of people who have encouraged and inspired me, and to whom I owe immense gratitude, must start with my family. Thanks to my amazing wife, Norah Martin, to my sons, Jake and Caleb, and to my parents and siblings, Hal and Virginia Pendergraft, Phil Pendergraft, and Vicki Taylor and their families. Also I owe so much to my beloved love circle, Tracey Snoyer, Lou Ann Bennett, Pat Wasp, and Phil and Heidi Evans. You challenge and inspire me constantly.

I have deep gratitude for my incredible editor, Ben Clemenzi-Allen, and his wonderful team, especially Olivia and Megan. Ben, this book would be so much less without you.

I have learned so much from my colleagues over the years at ProtoCall Services, VMC Behavioral Health, Magellan, and Lifetime Optimization. Particular thanks go to Kathleen Berman, Annette Adams, Jim Smith, Tammy Tone, Bob Cain, Kristin

Newby, Lindsay Branine, Brandt Rigby, Jeremy Koehler, and all the counselors and volunteers I had the privilege to work with at ProtoCall and Metro Crisis. Special thanks to the LTO team - Evan McGuirk, Leslie Prieto, Danielle Ross, and again, Jake and Caleb.

I am so grateful for my mentor, Steve Linder, and my SRI cabinet - Omer Ozden, Billy Bowden, Jo Formosa, Corey Cain, Kelly Haney, and Walker Wynkoop. You challenged me to step up my game and I had to live up to your belief in me. And my peers with SRI have always pushed me in the best way possible. Thank you Alex Changho, Bib Mohanty, Summer Rose, Chad Dymon, Joseph Hastreiter, Noreen Brower, Danielle Moniz, Lisa Cooney, Karen and Francisco, and so many more. You know who you are. So many of these friends also come from the Tony Robbins event environment, evidence of the impact he has had on so many. I will always be grateful to Tony for his inspiration and life changing strategies.

This book brought together two long-time loves— writing and helping people. Those of you who supported my writing go way back into the dim past, and you have shaped this book by influencing me as a person and a writer. I am grateful especially for the writing inspiration of Pamela Lancaster Elzinga, as well as for her lifetime friendship and that of Kevin Arps, Ric Telford, Chip Court, and Chuck and Linda Grady. Thank you, Liz Earnhart, you taught me so much. Special thanks to my first writing teachers, Bob Flynn and Dave Burkett.

More recently, my friends and colleagues Dick Eaton, Holly Hagerman, Kim LaFever, Dino Paris, and the whole business growth coaching group. How many times did one of you ask me, "So, when are you going to write that book?" I will always be thankful for the encouragement.

Thank you, Sandi Serling. May you activate happiness for so many people! Thank you, Mike Rohrig; without you I would never have become 'Brain Coach Brad.' Thank you Stuart Funke, you always remind me we are here to help people be free. Thank you, Kelsey Kiser. Thank you Vickie Burleigh. Thank you Julia Cronin for letting me share your story.

Finally, my deepest gratitude goes always to the clients I have had the privilege to help and to learn from. You remind me of my deepest purpose in this life—to bring joy and radiant love and to help as all break through our perceived limits. Keep on breaking through!

ABOUT THE AUTHOR

Having suffering tremendously with stress, worry, and anxiety himself, Brad Pendergraft found the most powerful way out of his struggles. He gained a deep understanding of the human brain and learned how to provide this understanding in the most effective ways to the greatest number of people. Brad is known as "Brain Coach Brad," a Licensed Clinical Social Worker, a Master Practitioner of NLP (neuro-linguistic programing), a certified hypnotherapist, a Life and Executive Coach, and the co-founder of a national crisis and trauma response company that served 500,000 calls in 2014 alone. In his clinical work, he has logged tens of thousands of hours, has trained thousands of clinicians, and counseled officers in the NYPD after the 9/11 crisis.

He can now be found working with clients across the globe, providing trainings for the world's best success coaches, turning neuroscience research into practical strategies, and speaking at major events.